Anonymous

Blue Book of Indianapolis

A social directory and club list forming a convenient guide for calls and parties, and

a select list for mailing purposes

Anonymous

Blue Book of Indianapolis
A social directory and club list forming a convenient guide for calls and parties, and a select list for mailing purposes

ISBN/EAN: 9783337289089

Printed in Europe, USA, Canada, Australia, Japan

Cover: Foto ©Suzi / pixelio.de

More available books at **www.hansebooks.com**

INDIANAPOLIS,

A SOCIAL DIRECTORY AND CLUB LIST,

FORMING A CONVENIENT GUIDE FOR CALLS AND
PARTIES, AND A SELECT LIST FOR
MAILING PURPOSES.

INDIANAPOLIS,
The Blue Book Publishing Co.,
1894.

ANNOUNCEMENT.

THE Publishers of this, the first Indianapolis Blue Book, have taken the greatest pains to make it an accurate and representative publication. That it contains errors we well know. Many intelligent people distrust a new departure and withhold information which is for the general good. But we feel sure the book will win its way. We will thank those who are interested in making it better to send in corrections at once. These will be embodied in a supplement to be issued about Jan. 1st, 1894, and mailed free to all subscribers.

Respectfully,
The Blue Book Pub. Co.

PRESS OF ....
    J. B. SAVAGE,
        .... CLEVELAND, O.

GENERAL INDEX.

	PAGE.
Art Association,	165
Boys' Home and Employment Association,	172
Century Club,	133
Clio Club,	135
College Corner Club,	136
Contemporary Club,	137
Deaf and Dumb Asylum,	173
Dramatic Club,	143
Flower Mission,	171
Fortnightly Literary Club,	146
Free Kindergarten,	176
Indiana Reform School for Girls,	174
Indianapolis Literary Club,	150
Indianapolis Propylæum,	153
Industrial School for Girls,	175
Katherine Merrill Club,	148
Katherine Home,	177
Ladies Matinee Musicale,	156
Local Council of Women,	178
Woman's Auxiliary to Y. M. C. A.,	179

INDEX TO STREETS.

Alabama Street,
Alabama Street, North,
Ash Street,
Broadway,
Central Avenue,
Christian Avenue,
College Avenue,
Delaware Street, North,
East Drive, (W. P.)
East Street, North,
Fletcher Avenue,
Home Avenue,
Illinois Street, North,
Meridian Street, North,
Michigan Street, East,
Michigan Street, West,
Middle Drive, (W. P.)
Mississippi Street, North,
Morrison Street,
New Jersey Street, North,
New York Street, East,

INDEX TO STREETS—Continued.

Ohio Street, East,
Ohio Street, West,
Park Avenue,
Pennsylvania Street, North,
Pratt Street, East,
Ruckle Street,
St. Clair Street, East,
St. Clair Street, West,
St. Joseph Street, East,
Talbott Avenue,
Tennessee Street, North,
Vermont Street, West,
Washington Street, East,
West Drive, (W. P.)
West Street, North,
West Second Street,
West Walnut Street,
Woodruff Place,

The Blue Book Publishing Co.

Cleveland, Detroit, Indianapolis.

Publishers of Blue Books of the above named Cities and Dealers in Blue Books of all Cities. . . .

ADDRESS

Blue Book Publishing Co.
Cleveland, Ohio.

Zumpfe's - Orchestra,

FURNISHES LATEST MUSIC FOR

Concerts, Receptions and Dances.

W. A. ZUMPFE, Leader.

Room 18, Insurance Blk.   N. E. Cor. Market and Penn. Sts.

NICKUM, CATERER,

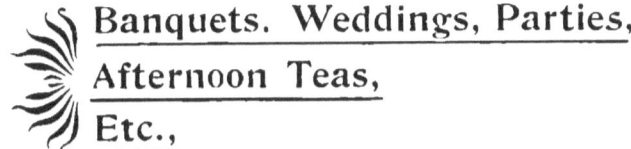

Banquets. Weddings, Parties, Afternoon Teas, Etc.,

Gotten up in first-class style. Menus furnished to any-one on application, free of charge.

75 Massachusetts Avenue,

INDIANAPOLIS, IND.

 PHOTOGRAPHER

OPPOSITE

BATES HOUSE.

Corner Illinois and Washington Sts.

Men's Tailoring.

OUR FACILITIES for first-class tailor work place us in the first rank. We employ

Only the Best Workmen,

and our cutters are artists in their profession.

It is unnecessary to enumerate the advantages of first-class Merchant Tailor work over ready made, and with our facilities the cost is but a trifle higher and the

Product is Perfect.

Other so-called Merchant Tailors may offer cheaper work, but it will not stand comparison with our out-put.

Business Suits, - - - $20 and upwards.
Overcoats, - - - - $20 " "
Dress Suits, evening wear for gentlemen $25 " "

Kahn Tailoring Company,

22 and 24 E. Washington St.

No Connection with any other House.

Ladies' Tailoring.

A year ago, recognizing the fact that the City of Indianapolis is of metropolitan size, and that its citizens demand the best of what is current elsewhere, we determined to open our

GOWNERY,

a department in which we would furnish Ladies' Tailoring, garments made to measure by men-tailors, under the supervision of a cutter who for years had direction of a large house of the kind in VIENNA, AUSTRIA, the most fashionable capital in Europe.

Each season we will have provided a great variety of the

Latest and Most Fashionable

Fabrics, which we are prepared to make up in the best metropolitan styles in Gowns, Jackets and Wraps of all kinds.

This is the only house of the kind in Indiana. Ladies invited to call.

Kahn Tailoring Company,

Correspondence Solicited.
Lady Attendant.

22 and 24 E. Washington St.

THE ESPECIAL ✢ CHARACTERISTICS

—OF—

Baldwin
PIANOS.

Perfect Scale, Beautiful and Rich Tone, Elastic and Responsive Touch, Greatest Durability and Capacity for Standing in Tune, Artistic Designs of Cases.

GENERAL FACTORS,

D. H. Baldwin & Co.,
95, 97 and 99 North Pennsylvania St.

Moving orders given prompt attention.
Tuning guaranteed. Storage at low prices, with insurance.

Alphabetical List.

ABBETT Chas. H., Mr. and Mrs......... 82 W. Vermont st.
Abbett Earnest Lawrence....... 82 W. Vermont st.
Adams George F., Mr. and Mrs......... 148 E. New York st.
Adams Lida, Miss........................... 148 E. New York st.
Adams Justus Cooley, Mr. and Mrs....... 750 N. Delaware st.
Adams Fred. Bliss............................750 N. Delaware st.
Adams Bertrand, Mr. and Mrs............ 765 N. Alabama st.
Adams Henry Clay, Mr. and Mrs......... 622 N. Alabama st.
Adams Henry Clay, Jr..................... 622 N. Alabama st.
Adams Elizabeth Brown, Mrs................ 211 Park ave.
Adams Isabell M. Mrs .... 277 N. Delaware st.
Adams Edith, Miss............................. 211 Park ave.
Adams Kate, Miss............................ 211 Park ave.
Adams Henry Alden........ .... 211 Park ave.
Adsit J. M. Mrs .... 861 N. Meridian st.
Ahern Nellie, Miss (Asst. State Libr.).... 331 N. N. Jersey.
Albrecht Maurice, Dr. and Mrs......78 Middle Drive (W. P.)
Aldag Harry W Mrs........ .... 583 E. Washington st.
Aldag Charles, Mr. and Mrs........... 644 E. Washington st.

Aldag Minnie, Miss. ...... 644 E. Washington st.
Aldag Cora, Miss ...... 644 E. Washington st.
Alexander Coke, Mr. and Mrs ...... 129 E. St. Joseph st.
Alexander Carrie, Mrs ...... 103 Meridian st.
Allen Wm. Chas., Mr. and Mrs ...... 280 N. N. Jersey st.
Allen Horace R., Dr. and Mrs ...... 679 N. Delaware st.
Allen Horace R., Jr. ...... 679 N. Delaware st.
Allen Henry Clay, Mr. and Mrs ...... 874 N. Alabama st.
Allen A. T., Mr. and Mrs ...... 270 N. Delaware st.
Allen Fredonia, Miss ...... 832 N. Pennsylvania st.
Allen Granville G., Mr. and Mrs ...... 449 Broadway.
Allison John A., Mr. and Mrs ...... 556 N. Illinois st.
Allison Wm., Dr. and Mrs ...... 328 Broadway.
Anderson James S., Mr. and Mrs ...... 296 N. Illinois st.
Anderson Stella, Mrs ...... 390 N. Delaware st.
Anderson Fidelia, Miss ...... 307 N. Delaware st.
Aneshaeusel Charles, Mr. and Mrs ... 359 Park ave. (Thurs.)
Anthony George, Mr ...... 326 N. Meridian st.
Anthony Grove, Dr ...... 310 North East.
Anthony Emanuel, Dr. and Mrs ...... 310 North East.
Appel Daniel Fred, Mr. and Mrs ...... 777 N. Meridian st.
Appel John J., Mr. and Mrs ...... 387 Broadway.
Applegate Wm. A., Mr. and Mrs ...... 28 Central ave.
Applegate Wm. H ...... 28 Central ave.
Applegate Berg ...... 274 N. Jersey st.
Arms Frank X., Mr. and Mrs ...... 439 N. N. Jersey st.
Armstrong Frank W., Mr. and Mrs ...... 396 Broadway.
Atkins Edward Cornelius, Mr. and Mrs..666 N. Meridian st.
Atkins Laura Francis, Miss ...... 666 N. Meridian st.
Atkins Emma Louise, Miss ...... 666 N. Meridian st.
Atkins Henry C., Mr ...... 666 N. Meridian st.

Atkins George W., Mr. and Mrs...... 577 N. Mississippi st.
Austin Augusta, Miss ....31 W. Pratt st.
Ayler Margaret, Mrs................... 359 N. Pennsylvania st.
Ayres Lyman S., Mr. and Mrs............656 N. Delaware st.
Ayres Fred M., Mr...... ....656 N. Delaware st.
Ayres Alexander C., Mr. and Mrs......31 W. Drive, (W. P.)
Ayres Ida, Miss ....31 W. Drive, (W. P.)

B ABB Grace Gilman, Miss...........621 N. Tennessee st.
Bachus Victor, Mr. and Mrs.........775 Meridian st.
Bacon Duncan, Mr. and Mrs..................71 W. Vermont st.
Baggs Frederick, Mr. and Mrs..... ....100 Alabama st.
Baggs Thomas B., Mr........................... 100 Alabama st.
Bahr Paul, Mr. and Mrs.................572 E. Washington st.
Bahr Clara, Miss ....572 E. Washington st.
Bahr Max, Mr......................... .... 572 E. Washington st.
Bailey Owen R., Mr................. ....340 N. Meridian st.
Bailey Leon O., Mr........... .... Grand Hotel.
Bailey Frederick W....................................Grand Hotel.
Bain James Edward, Mr. and Mrs......127 E. St. Joseph st.
Bain Bessie Louise, Miss................ 127 E. St. Joseph st.
Bain Harry Clegg, Mr.....................127 E. St. Joseph st.
Baird John W., Mr. and Mrs...................33 Christian ave.
Baker Braxton, Mr. and Mrs.....................370 Park ave.
Baker A. R. Mrs ....48 West st.
Baker Alberta, Miss........................ 48 West st.
Baker Wm. L. Mr. and Mrs.................... ..440 Park ave.
Baker J. H., Judge and Mrs................ ."The Denison."
Baker Charlotte, Mrs........................ 350 Park ave.
Baker Alice, Miss ....350 Park ave.

Baldwin James H., Mr. and Mrs....385 N. Pennsylvania st.
Baldwin Margaret, Miss..............385 N. Pennsylvania st.
Baldwin Silas, Mr. and Mrs..............440 N. Meridian st.
Baldwin Anna Belle, Miss....... { ..385 N. Pennsylvania st. / Harbor Point Mich.
Ballard Granville, Mr. and Mrs............293 N. Meridian st.
Ballard Lucile, Miss......................293 N. Meridian st.
Ballard Harrison, Mr. and Mrs............287 N. Meridian st.
Bank Samuel E., Mr. and Mrs............167 N. Alabama st.
Banning James H., Mr. and Mrs..University and Ritter aves.
Baugher Leigh R., Mr. and Mrs..........783 N. Delaware st.
Barbour Harriet, Mrs....................621 N. Tennessee st.
Barcus James Q., Mr. and Mrs...................381 Broadway.
Baris Lina, Miss.................866 N. Pennsylvania st.
Barkley Wm. L, Mr. and Mrs............251 N. Meridian st.
Barkley Merrill B.......................... .251 N. Meridian st.
Barkley Douglas J..............................251 N. Meridian st.
Barney Chester, Mr. and Mrs............180 E. Drive, (W. P.)
Barney George L., Mr. and Mrs..........28 N. Drive, (W. P.)
Barnes Dawson, Dr. and Mrs..............213 N. Illinois st.
Barnes Carl, Dr....................213 N. Illinois st.
Barnes Carl, Mr. and Mrs..................243 N. East st.
Barnes Albert, Mr. and Mrs..................782 N. Illinois st.
Barnard J. A., Mr..........................."The Denison."
Barnett John T., Mr. and Mrs ....623 N. Meridian st.
Barnhill J. F., Dr. and Mrs...................... Central ave.
Barry Wm. B., Mr. and Mrs.....................224 College ave.
Barry Thomas, Mr. and Mrs.................553 N. Meridian st.
Barry Margaret, Miss..................553 N. Meridian st.
Basler Agnes, Mrs........................849 N. Illinois st.
Bassett Thomas, Mr. and Mrs.......599 N. Pennsylvania st.

THE ELITE LIST.

Bates Henry, Mr. and Mrs......................"Bates House."
Bates Henry, Jr. and Mrs................316 N. Meridian st.
Beck George C., Mr. and Mrs.............635 N. Meridian st.
Beck Bessie, Miss............................635 N. Meridian st.
Beck George A., Mr.........................635 N. Meridian st.
Beck A. T., Mr.................................."The Denison."
Beck Wm. S., Dr. and Mrs................863 N. Meridian st.
Beck Harry Abraham........................863 N. Meridian st.
Behm George H., Mr. and Mrs ....388 Park ave.
Belitz Adolph, Dr. and Mrs....................282 Central ave.
Belcher Thos. W. S., Mr. and Mrs.... 147 N. Pennsylvania st.
Bell Allen, Mr. and Mrs.......................221 Christian ave.
Bell Jessie, Miss...............................221 Christian ave.
Bellis Wm. K., Mr. and Mrs................564 N. Meridian st.
Bennett Henry W., Mr. and Mrs.........241 N. Meridian st.
Bennett Horace T.......................765 N. Pennsylvania st.
Benson Adelbert, Mr. and Mrs............876 N. Delaware st.
Benson Luther, Mr. and Mrs.............873 N. Delaware st.
Benton George, Mr.......................420 N. Pennsylvania st.
Benton Howard, Mr. and Mrs...............855 N. Meridian st.
Benton Eliza, Miss................................20 E. Pratt st.
Bessonies August, Rt. Rev....cor. N. Meridian and 5th sts.
Beveridge Albert J., Mr. and Mrs ....30 Christian ave.
Bicknell Earnest P., Mr. and Mrs.................64 Ruckle st.
Binford Mary Augusta, Mrs..................556 N. Illinois st.
Bingham Joseph J., Mr. and Mrs.........546 N. Meridian st.
Bingham F. L., Mr............. ....546 N. Meridian st.
Bingham Edmund, Mr......................546 N. Meridian st.
Bingham Emily S. Miss ....546 N. Meridian st.
Bingham Laura M. Miss .... 546 N. Meridian st.
Bingham George W., Mr. and Mrs...146 E. Drive, (W. P.)

Bird Frank, Mr. and Mrs.....................683 N. Illinois st.
Bird Jessie, Miss..................................683 N. Illinois st.
Black James, Judge and Mrs...........399 N. Pennsylvania st.
Black Charles H................................247 E. Louisiana ave.
Blackman Clarence, Mr. and Mrs................120 E. 6th st.
Blackledge Albert S.............................975 N. Meridian st.
Blackledge John W..............................975 N. Meridian st.
Blackledge Susan K.............................975 N. Meridian st.
Blackledge Irene L..............................975 N. Meridian st.
Blackledge Frank H., Mr. and Mrs........... 205 N. East st.
Blair Aaron H., Mr. and Mrs..............581 N. Delaware st.
Blaker Louis, Mr. and Mrs.............1196 N. Meridian ave.
Blanchard Frank A., Mr. and Mrs..272 N. Pennsylvania st.
Blanton Emma, Mrs.....................................27 E. 2d st.
Blanton Llewellyn........................596 N. Pennsylvania st.
Bliss George, Mr. and Mrs..................455 N. Tennessee st.
Bliss Henry, Mr. and Mrs.....................16 W. Drive, (W. P.)
Blizzard Wm., Mr. and Mrs.................519 W. Meridian st.
Blodgett Wm. H., Mr. and Mrs..........963 N. Tennessee st.
Bloomer Isaac L., Mr. and Mrs......457 N. Pennsylvania st.
Bloomer Ashael...............................457 N. Pennsylvania st.
Blount Brazilia, Rev. and Mrs.........Washington, Irvington.
Blount Sadie, Miss..........................Washington, Irvington.
Blount Grace, Miss.........................Washington, Irvington.
Blount Willis ....Washington, Irvington.
Blount B. M., Mr. and Mrs.............Washington, Irvington.
Bobbs Wm. C., Mr. and Mrs.........................440 Broadway.
Boggs Anna, Mrs............................735 N. Pennsylvania st.
Bohlen Oscar D., Mr. and Mrs.....................350 Broadway.
Bohlen Frances, Mrs....................................412 Broadway.
Boice Augustin, Mr. and Mrs...................678 Delaware st.

THE ELITE LIST.

Bond Mary, Mrs..164 Broadway.
Bond Mary E., Miss......................................164 Broadway.
Bond Pleasant, Mr. and Mrs.........................446 Park ave.
Boothby Arthur, Mr. and Mrs.....................178 Christian ave.
Borgundthal David C., Mr. and Mrs.........313 W. North st.
Bosson Wm., Mr. and Mrs..Mapleton.
Bowen Silas T., Mr. and Mrs.......................44 W. North st.
Bowles Kate Moore, Mrs...............................493 N. Meridian st.
Bowles Joseph, Mr ....493 N. Meridian st.
Bowles Duane, Mr..493 N. Meridian st.
Bowles Osborne, Mr..493 N. Meridian st.
Boyd Lawson, Mr. and Mrs..........................393 Broadway.
Boyle Lewis V., Mr. and Mrs.......................354 College st.
Boyles Ellen, Miss..............................Grand ave., Irvington.
Boyles Carrie, Miss............................Grand ave., Irvington.
Bradbury Geo. L., Mr......................................"The Denison."
Bradbury Daniel M., Mr. and Mrs..............308 Home.
Braden David, Mr. and Mrs.........................978 N. Tennessee st.
Bradford Wm. B., Mr. and Mrs...................700 N. Meridian st.
Bradford Chester, Mr. and Mrs...................1088 N. Illinois st.
Bradshaw John A., Mr. and Mrs.................26 E. Vermont st.
Bradshaw John E., Mr....................................515 N. Pennsylvania st.
Branham Geo. F., Mr. and Mrs....................119 E. Michigan st.
Branham Geo. E..119 E. Michigan st.
Branton Frances, Miss....................................525 Broadway.
Brayton Alembert, Dr. and Mrs..................808 E. Washington st.
Brazington Wm. C., Mr ....673 N. Meridian st.
Brennan E. J., Dr. and Mrs..........................240 N. Tennessee st.
Brennan Vincent Graham..............................240 N. Tennessee st.
Brink Christian, Mr..333 N. Tennessee st.
Brink Matilda, Miss...333 N. Tennessee st.

Brink Louise C., Miss ....333 N. Tennessee st.
Bristor Wm. Albert, Mr. and Mrs......560 N. Tennessee st.
Bristor Burton, Miss ....560 N. Tennessee st.
Broden James, Mr. and Mrs............271 E. New York st.
Broden James, Jr..........................271 E. New York st.
Bronson Henry Martin, Mr. and Mrs...225 N. Tennessee st.
Bronson Frank Ferris....................225 N. Tennessee st.
Bronson Chas. S., Mr. and Mrs.....63 Middle Drive, (W. P.)
Brouse Charles Wm................University ave., Irvington.
Brouse Mary Thorpe, Miss ......University ave , Irvington.
Brouse Louise, Miss ....University ave., Irvington.
Brown Wm. Thos., Mr. and Mrs.................291 Park ave.
Brown Edgar A., Judge and Mrs ....200 Broadway.
Brown Chalmers, Mr ....564 N. Meridian st.
Brown Jesse H...............................421 N. Meridian st.
Brown Herbert H............................421 N. Meridian st.
Brown Demarcus C........................ University ave. Irv.
Brown Hilton W., Mr. and Mrs.. . ...361 Massachusetts st.
Brown Wm. R., Mr. and Mrs........859 N. Pennsylvania st.
Brown John R., Dr. and Mrs..............102 N. Alabama st.
Brown Austin, Mr. and Mrs...............330 N. Meridian st.
Brown Wm. J., Mr. and Mrs..............448 N. Meridian st.
Brown Marcus L., Mr. and Mrs.........996 N. Tennessee st.
Brown Wm. H., Mr. and Mrs..............280 N. Meridian st.
Browne Joseph, Mr. and Mrs.......... .43 W. Drive, (W. P.)
Browning Robert, Mr. and Mrs.............. 380 N. Illinois st.
Browning Henry L., Mr. and Mrs..... 631 N. Tennessee st.
Browning Eliza G. Miss..................631 N. Tennessee st.
Browning Wm. J. Dr......................631 N. Tennessee st.
Browning Corene T., Mrs.. .... 20 East Pratt st.
Bryan James W., Mr. and Mrs...............748 N. Illinois st.

Bryan Hugh, Mr.. 748 N. Illinois st.
Bryant Miss..384 N. Tennessee st.
Bryant Edwin Douglas, Mr. and Mrs......126 Michigan ave.
Bryant John W., Mr. and Mrs............384 N. Tennessee st.
Buchanan Anna, Mrs ....23 S. Alabama st.
Buchanan Fred M., Mr. and Mrs........670 N. Meridian st.
Buchanan Albert Edward, Mr. and Mrs.....950 N. Penn. st.
Buck George C., Mr. and Mrs...............574 College ave.
Buck Maude, Miss ....574 College ave.
Buchtel Henry A., Mr. and Mrs..............825 College ave.
Buchtel Frost Croft, Mr......................... 825 College ave.
Budd Wm. S., Mr. and Mrs.....................274 Central ave.
Budd Rose Martha, Miss.......................274 Central ave.
Budd John, Mr. and Mrs............................364 Park ave.
Buergeler Joseph, Mr. and Mrs............762 S. Meridian st.
Bufkin Sam., Mr. and Mrs....................315 N. Meridian st.
Bufkin Pearl, Miss........................ . 315 N. Meridian st.
Bundy Chas., Mr........................462 N. Pennsylvania st.
Burdsal Thos., Mr. and Mrs............... 545 N. Meridian st.
Burdsal Olive, Miss..............................545 N. Meridian st.
Burgess Chapin, Dr. and Mrs............1085 N. Tennessee st.
Burke Frederick M., Mr. and Mrs................8 Sterling st.
Burt Francis, Mr. and Mrs........................47 W. Drive, W. P.
Burford N. J., Mr. and Mrs................162 N. Meridian st.
Burford Wesley B.............................162 N. Meridian st.
Burford John T., Mr......................... 162 N. Meridian st.
Burford W. B., Mr. and Mrs...............700 N. Meridian st.
Buskirk Edward C., Mr. and Mrs..............116 Ruckle st.
Bush Frederick, Mr. and Mrs............451 N. Tennessee st.
Buskirk Geo. A., Mr. and Mrs..........961 N. Tennessee st.
Butler Scott, Mr. and Mrs............Downey ave., Irvington.

Butler Scott John .... Downey ave., Irvington.
Butler George Elgin .... Downey ave., Irvington.
Butler Eva Mitchell .... Downey ave., Irvington.
Butler Noble C., Mr. and Mrs .... 210 Park ave.
Butler Mary Browning, Miss .... 210 Park ave.
Butler John A., Mr .... 210 Park ave.
Butler Chauncy, Mr. and Mrs ..... 107 Middle Drive, (W. P.)
Butler Bessie, Miss .... 107 Middle Drive, (W. P.)
Butler Mahlon, Mr. and Mrs .... 306 N. Delaware st.
Butler Samuel Lee .... 306 N. Delaware st.
Butler John M., Mr. and Mrs .... 606 N. Delaware st.
Butler John Maurice .... 606 N. Delaware st.
Butler Ovid, Mr. and Mrs .... 768 N. Pennsylvania st.
Butler D. W., Mrs .... 765 N. Pennsylvania st. (Tuesday.)
Butler Henry, Mr. and Mrs .... 448 College ave.
Butterfield Webster, Dr. and Mrs .... 366 N. East st.
Bybee Addison, Mr. and Mrs .... 625 N. Pennsylvania st.
Bybee Jessie, Miss .... 625 N. Pennsylvania st.
Bybee Alice, Miss .... 625 N. Pennsylvania st.
Bynum Wm. D., Mr. and Mrs .... 411 Ash st.
Byfield Charles W., Mr .... 909 N. Illinois st.
Byfield Arthur H .... 909 N. Illinois st.
Byfield Harry N .... 909 N. Illinois st.
Byfield Bessie C .... 909 N. Illinois st.
Byfield Emma C .... 909 N. Illinois st.
Byram Oliver T .... 956 N. Illinois st.
Byram Henry G .... 956 N. Illinois st.
Byram Norman S .... 956 N. Illinois st.

THE ELITE LIST.

CADY Fred. Wilbur, Mr. and Mrs..11 W. Division (W. P.)
Caldwell, Miss ....785 N. Pennsylvania st.
Cale Howard, Mr. and Mrs......................492 Broadway.
Calkins Mary, Mrs.....................Downey ave., Irvington.
Carey John Newman, Mr. and Mrs......660 N. Meridian st.
Carey Lowe, Mr. and Mrs..................34 W. St. Joseph st.
Carey Harvey G., Mr............................... 48 W. North st.
Carey Mary, Mrs............. .... 48 W. North st.
Carey Maria Fletcher............. ....48 W. North st.
Carleton George, Mr....................738 N. Pennsylvania st.
Carleton Fannie, Miss............. ...738 N. Pennsylvania st.
Carnahan James R , Mr. and Mrs........8 W. Drive, (W. P.)
Carnahan, Miss..................................8 W. Drive, (W. P.)
Carr Michael W., Mr. and Mrs.................... 579 Park ave.
Carr Reed............... ......282 N. Pennsylvania st.
Carson John F., Mr. and Mrs......831 N. Penn. (Tuesday).
Carson Edward, Mr.....................831 N. Pennsylvania st.
Carstensen Gustav A., Rev. and Mrs.739 Penn. (Tuesday).
Carter George, Mr. and Mrs..................... 72 W. Second st.
Carter Vinson, Mr. and Mrs......... 582 N. Pennsylvania st.
Carter Anna Louise, Miss......... ...582 N. Pennsylvania st.
Carvin Orville, Mr. and Mrs.........Washington, Irvington.
Cary Elmer E., Dr. and Mrs..................151 N. Illinois st.
Cathcart Robert W., Mr. and Mrs..439 N. Pennsylvania st.
Catherwood Ellen, Mrs ....438 N. Meridian st.
Catherwood Mary, Miss.................. 438 N. Meridian st.
Catterson George N., Mr. and Mrs..808 Meridian (Monday)
Chambers Smiley, Mr. and Mrs...........771 N. Alabama st.
Chambers James, Mr. and Mrs...............174 Fletcher ave.
Chambers Eleanora E., Mrs................640 N. Illinois st.

Chandler Thomas E., Mr. and Mrs .....284 W. Vermont st.
Chapman Page, Mr....................19 W. Drive, (W. P.)
Chardrand Joseph, Rev............Cor. Meridian and 5th st.
Chase Ira J., Rev. and Mrs ....Irvington.
Chase, Miss..Irvington.
Chase, Mr..Irvington.
Chase Lecia, Miss....................................Irvington.
Chasard, F. S., Rev................cor. Meridian and 5th sts.
Chestnutt John, Mr. and Mrs..............814 N. Alabama st.
Chislett Frederick W., Mr. and Mrs...............Crown Hill.
Chislett John, Mr...............................Crown Hill.
Chislett Frederick, Mr. and Mrs............575 N. Illinois st.
Chislett Richard Edward, Mr. and Mrs ......71 Talbott ave.
Christian John E., Mr. and Mrs.............. 137 E. Pratt st.
Christian Thomas J............................74 W. Walnut st.
Christian Wilmer F., Mr. and Mrs ..... 206 N. Alabama st.
Christian Harry E........................206 N. Alabama st.
Christian Wilmer F. Jr....................206 N. Alabama st.
Clarke Chas. Burres, Mr. and Mrs..Central ave., Irvington.
Clayton Rena, Miss.........................782 N. Illinois st.
Claypool Solomon, Judge and Mrs . .....1088 N. Illinois st.
Claypool John Wilson, Mr................. 1088 N. Illinois st.
Claypool Edward T., Mr. and Mrs........182 N. Meridian st.
  Summer Res., Claypool Villa, Martha's Vineyard, Mass.
Claypool Anna L., Mrs........................24 Home ave.
Cleland Harriet, Miss.....................32 West St. Clair st.
Cleland John E., Mr. and Mrs ....32 West St. Clair st.
Clemmer Fred. O., Dr. and Mrs......... 525 N. Delaware st.
Cleveland Horace Agard, Rev. and Mrs...35 W. N. York st.
Cleveland Eleanor A., Mrs................35 W. New York st.
Clifford Vincent G., Mr....................347 N. Illinois st.

Cline L. C., Dr. and Mrs....................862 N. Meridian st.
Clippenger Jessie, Miss............................24 Home ave.
Clune John, Mr. and Mrs..................1022 N. Meridian st.
Clune, Miss....................................1022 N. Meridian st.
Clune Michael, Mr. and Mrs..........619 N. Pennsylvania st.
Clune Anna, Miss ....619 N. Pennsylvania st.
Clune Wm. J............................. 619 N. Pennsylvania st.
Coburn Willard Henry, Mr. and Mrs...874 N. Delaware st.
Coburn Henry, Mr. and Mrs.................121 E. New York st.
Coburn Wm. H., Mr. and Mrs............121 E. New York st.
Coburn Henry, Jr ....121 E. New York st.
Coburn John, Mr. and Mrs........................40 Hendricks st.
Coburn Augustus, Mr. and Mrs......887 N. Pennsylvania st.
Cochrum John B., Mr. and Mrs................311 College ave.
Coe Henry, Mr. and Mrs......................277 N. Delaware st.
Coe Charles B., Mrs..............................110 Talbott ave.
Coe Anna May, Miss.............................110 Talbott ave.
Coffin Chas. E., Mr. and Mrs ....800 N. Pennsylvania ave.
Coffin Percival B., Mr. and Mrs..........996 N. Tennessee st.
Coffin Frank A., Mr. and Mrs............. 510 N. Delaware st.
Coffin David W., Mr. and Mrs .... 854 N. Meridian st.
Coffin Florence North, Miss........ ......854 N. Meridian st.
Coffin Albert W., Mr. and Mrs....................393 Park ave.
Coldwell Horace G., Mr. and Mrs....147 East Drive, (W. P.)
Coleman Wm. H., Mr. and Mrs...............34 W. Second st.
Coleman John A., Mr. and Mrs ....366 Alabama st.
Cole Blanche, Miss. ....424 N. Meridian st.
Cole Barton W., Mr. and Mrs ....388 Broadway.
Colgan Henrietta, Miss.............................298 Park ave.
Colgan Mary, Miss...................................298 Park ave.
Collins Samuel H., Mr. and Mrs.......... 128 N. Meridian st.

Comstock Albert S., Mr. and Mrs............790 Meridian st.
Comstock Chas. H., Mr. and Mrs.........429 N. Delaware st.
Combs Dr. G. W...............................''The Dennison.''
Commons John M., Mr. and Mrs................210 Broadway.
Compton Samuel, Mr. and Mrs............172 N. Delaware st.
Conde Henry T., Mr. and Mrs....................210 Broadway.
Conduit Allen, Mr. and Mrs.......................380 Park ave.
Conduit Mabel Miss..................................380 Park ave.
Conner John B., Mr. and Mrs....................360 Park ave.
Conner Adah, Miss ....360 Park ave.
Consingor J. A., Dr. and Mrs ....520 N. Illinois st.
Cooper John J., Mr. and Mrs..............400 N. Meridian st.
Cooper Chas. M., Mr ....400 N. Meridian st.
Cooper Wm. H., Mr. and Mrs............181 N. Tennessee st.
Cooper Wm., Mr................................181 N. Tennessee st.
Cooper Wm. Dawson, Mr. and Mrs............350 College ave.
Cooper Elizabeth Ingram, Miss...............350 College ave.
Cooper Lew. Wallace, Mr. and Mrs ....342 Broadway.
Cooper George Pearson, Mr. and Mrs..863 N. Delaware st.
Cook Wm. H., Mr. and Mrs................705 N. Alabama st.
Cookus John T., Mr. and Mrs.................24 W. North st.
Cookus Nellie, Miss...............................24 W. North st.
Cookus Lillie, Miss................................24 W. North st.
Coons John Wm., Mr. and Mrs...........872 N. Alabama st.
Cottman George S., Mr............University ave., Irvington.
Cornelius Edward G., Mr. and Mrs.........25 W. Walnut st.
Cornelius Sadie Willis, Miss ....25 W. Walnut st.
Coughlen Harry G., Mr. and Mrs......799 N. Tennessee st.
Coughlen Wm., Mr. and Mrs......... 400 N. Tennessee st.
Coughlen Mary, Miss...........................400 N. Tennessee st.
Coughlen Frank W.............................400 N. Tennessee st.

Coughlen Wm. F., Mr.................... 400 N. Tennessee st.
Coughlen Edward, Dr...................... 400 N. Tennessee st.
Cowan Wm. A., Mr. and Mrs................. 63 Nordyke ave.
Cowan John, Mr............................ 272 N. Meridian st.
Cox Linton Alden, Mr. and Mrs.......... 302 N. Delaware st.
Cox Millard, Mr. and Mrs........ 636 N. Alabama st. (Thur.)
Cox Harriet, Mrs....................... 580 Alabama st.
Cox David, Mr. and Mrs.............. 564 N. Pennsylvania st.
Crandall Joseph, Mr. and Mrs............ 894 N. Illinois st.
Craig John A............................. 482 N. Illinois st.
Craig Charles, Mr..................... 482 N. Illinois st.
Craft Richard P................ .... 897 N. Delaware st.
Crossland Harry A., Mr. and Mrs......... 768 N. Alabama st.
Cropsey James M., Mr. and Mrs............. 235 College ave.
Cropsey Nebraska, Miss. .... 235 College ave.
Crowell Melvin E., Mr................. 339 N. Pennsylvania st.
Croxall Blanche, Miss.......................... Blind Asylum.
Curtis James B., Mr. and Mrs........ 616 N. Pennsylvania st.
Cutter Frank C., Mr........................ 640 N. Illinois st.
Culbertson Chas. A., Mr. and Mrs.......... 185 St. Mary's st.
Curtis Edward, Rev. and Mrs.............. 452 N. Delaware st.
Cutter Fred. P., Mr. and Mrs............... 640 N. Illinois st.
Cutting John Andrew, Mr. and Mrs........ 894 N. Illinois st.
Cummings Matthew, Mr. and Mrs.............. 320 Park ave.
Cullen Terry J., Mr. and Mrs............. 422 N. Meridian st.
Crouse Jeanette, Miss......................... 37 Park ave.
Crouse Francis M..................... .... 37 Park ave.
Cross Chas. M., Mr. and Mrs........... Ritter ave., Irvington.
Cutter Florence E., Miss.................... 640 N. Illinois st.
Cutter Frederick Page..................... 640 N. Illinois st

DAGGETT Wm., Mr. and Mrs...280 N. New Jersey st.
Daggett Cora Olive, Miss .....280 N. New Jersey st.
Daggett Wm. H., Mr. and Mrs.............136 Maryland st.
Dale Oliver S., Mr. and Mrs.................432 Central ave.
Dale Burnham C., Mr........................432 Central ave.
Dalton Nathan F., Mr. and Mrs...........208 N. Alabama st.
Dalton Charles Mr.........................208 N. Alabama st.
Dalrymple John W., Mr. and Mrs..............183 Park ave.
Dalrymple Helen, Miss......................183 Park ave.
Daniels Edward, Mr. and Mrs.......883 N. Pennsylvania st.
Dark Charles E., Mr. and Mrs............512 N. Meridian st.
Dark Edward, Mr.........................512 N. Meridian st.
Dark Wilbur, Mr.........................512 N. Meridian st.
Darlington Frank Graves, Mr. and Mrs...676 N. Delaware st.
Dashiel John W., Rev. and Mrs...........683 N. Alabama st.
Daugherty E. J., Mr. and Mrs ...."The Denison."
Daugherty J. H., Dr. and Mrs ....Irvington.
Davis Frederick A., Mr. and Mrs.........677 N. Alabama st.
Davis G......................................677 N. Alabama st.
Davis Lusette, Miss........................677 N. Alabama st.
Davis Amanda J. Mrs......................776 N. Illinois st.
Davidson Walter, Mr......................47 Woodruff Place.
Dawson Richard Lew, Mr...........................53 Ruckle st.
Day Henry, Rev.........................122 N. Pennsylvania st.
Day Henry McCarty, Mr...............122 N. Pennsylvania st.
Day Margaret, Miss....................122 N. Pennsylvania st.
Day T. C., Mr. and Mrs...................820 N. Meridian st.
Day Florence, Miss........................820 N. Meridian st.
Dean Ward Hunt, Mr. and Mrs.....600 N. Pennsylvania st.
Dean Harriet R., Mrs....................620 N. Meridian st.

Dean Stewart, Mr............................620 N. Meridian st.
Dean Mary, Miss............................620 N. Meridian st.
Dean Wilfred, Mr.,............................620 N. Meridian st.
Dean Thomas, Mr. and Mrs..............573 N. Tennessee st.
Dean John Kingsbury, Mr................573 N. Tennessee st.
Dean Chas. Gilbert, Mr....................573 N. Tennessee st.
Dean Edward H., Mr. and Mrs..............355 Madison ave.
Dean John Candee, Mr................. 571 N. Pennsylvania st.
Dean Lillian Wright, Mrs......................81 W. Walnut st.
Dearborn Anna B., Mrs............................116 Park ave.
Dearborn Miss............................116 Park ave.
Dearborn Clair S., Mr............................116 Park ave.
Decker Albert Jackson, Mr. and Mrs........489 Meridian st.
Defrees Morris M., Mr. and Mrs..........74 W. Michigan st.
Defrees Fred., Mr............................. 74 W. Michigan st.
Denny Caleb S., Mr. and Mrs......... 673 N. Pennsylvania st.
Denny Mary, Miss...................... 673 N. Pennsylvania st.
Denny Carrie, Miss....................673 N. Pennsylvania st.
Denhurst Frederick E., Rev................665 N. Delaware st.
DeMotte Wm. H., Mr....................800 E. Washington st.
Demree Violette, Miss...........................51 Huron st.
DeRuiter Derk, Mr. and Mrs............ 1026 N. Meridian st.
Dewenter Herman, Mr. and Mrs..........698 N. Alabama st.
Dewenter Millie, Miss......................698 N. Alabama st.
DeWitt Carroll L., Mr..........................556 N. Illinois st.
Deschler Louis G., Mr. and Mrs.....789 N. Pennsylvania st.
DeSouchet Augustus M., Mr. and Mrs..297 N. Delaware st.
Dickerson Henry L., Rev. and Mrs........108 Lexington st.
Dickson Wm. C., Mr. and Mrs......474 N. Pennsylvania st.
Dickson Emma, Miss................... 474 N. Pennsylvania st.
Dickson James, Mr. and Mrs.....................240 N. East st.

Dickson Geo. A., Mr. and Mrs....... 644 N. Pennsylvania st.
Dickson John L., Mr. and Mrs....... 644 N. Pennsylvania st.
Dickinson Elizabeth R., Mrs......... 331 N. Pennsylvania st.
Dickinson Alice E....................... 331 N. Pennsylvania st.
Dickinson Jennie E..................... 331 N. Pennsylvania st.
Dietrich Margaret, Mrs............... 335 N. Pennsylvania st.
Dietrich Nettie, Miss...................335 N. Pennsylvania st.
Dietrich August, Mr. and Mrs...............435 Central ave.
Dilks John H., Mr...................... 203 N. Pennsylvania st.
Dilks Agnes Hyland................... 203 N. Penn ylvania st.
Dilks Nellie Eleanor.................... 203 N. Pennsylvania st.
Dill Howard Albert, Mr. and Mrs... 429 N. Pennsylvania st.
Dittemore John W., Mr.......................18 Central ave.
Dittemore Mabelle, Miss.........................18 Central ave.
Dodd John Wade, Mr. and Mrs...............476 N. Illinois st.
Doherty Charles J......................................The Denison.
Donley Edward, Mr. and Mrs...............122 W. Second st.
Donley Wm. Henry, Mr. and Mrs.........122 W. Second st.
Dollens Harry C., Mr..........................398 N. Illinois st.
Dollens Robert W., Mr. and Mrs...........398 N. Illinois st.
Donnan Barbara, Mrs......................126 N. Tennessee st.
Donnan Emma, Miss.......................126 N. Tennessee st.
Donnan Laura, Miss........................126 N. Tennessee st.
Donnan Theodore, Mr.....................126 N. Tennessee st.
Dorsey Daniel L., Mr.........................223 Central ave.
Dorsey Robert L., Mr. and Mrs..............233 Central ave.
Dorsey Katherine L., Mrs......................233 Central ave.
Dorsey Frank O ....233 Central ave.
Dorland Anna, Mrs..................... 129 N. Pennsylvania st.
Downing M. A., Mr. and Mrs............ 224 N. Meridian st.
Drew Harry E., Mr. and Mrs....... 705 N. Pennsylvania st.

Dryer Charles A., Mr. and Mrs..............368 Central ave.
Dudbridge S. B.,Mr. and Mrs...... 201 N. Pennsylvania st.
Duncan John S., Mr..........................672 N. Alabama st.
Duncan Agnes, Miss..........................672 N. Alabama st.
Duncan Wallace..............................672 N. Alabama st.
Dunlap Diantha, Mrs.........................600 N. Alabama st.
Dunlap Elizabeth, Miss......................600 N. Alabama st.
Dunlap Livingston...........................600 N. Alabama st.
Dunlap Wm. L., Mr. and Mrs..................639 N. Illinois st.
Dunn Jacob Piatt, Mr. and Mrs....467 N. Pennsylvania st.
Duzan Ada, Mrs........................ .. 858 N. Pennsylvania st.
Dunning Lehman, Dr. and Mrs................373 Broadway.
Dye Charity, Miss...........................188 Broadway.
Dye May, Miss.......... ....188 Broadway.
Dye John T., Mr. and Mrs....................599 N. Delaware st.
Dye Annie, Miss.............................599 N. Delaware st.
Dye Elizabeth F., Miss......................599 N. Delaware st.
Dye Maizie Bacon............................599 N. Delaware st.
Dyer Sidney M., Mr. and Mrs.................48 W. 12th st.
Dye Wm. Holton, Mr. and Mrs ....29 Morrison st.

EAGLESFIELD James T., Mr. and Mrs....527 Ash st.
Eastman Joseph, Dr. and Mrs...195 N. Delaware st.
Eastman Joseph Rilus, Mr..................195 N. Delaware st
Eastman Thomas, Dr. and Mrs............195 N. Delaware st.
Eastman Mary, Miss........................195 N. Delaware st.
Eastman Walter H., Mr. and Mrs.......750 N. Meridian st.
Eaton Helen A., Mrs.........................90 W. Walnut st.
Edson Hanford A., Mr. and Mrs... 422 N. Pennsylvania st.
Edson Ora, Miss............................206 Christian ave.
Edenharter Geo. F., Dr. and Mrs...City Hospital, Penn st.

Eddy Horace J., Mr. and Mrs..........56 W. Drive, (W. P.)
Edwards Alice, Miss................................Crown Hill.
Edwards, D. W., Mr. and Mrs.............248 Talbott ave.
Egan Edward Charles, Mr. and Mrs.....661 N. Meridian st.
Eitel Henry, Mr. and Mrs...................853 N. Meridian st.
Elam John B., Mr. and Mrs.......................300 Park ave.
Elder Margaretta S......................26 E. Vermont st.
Elder Wm. Line, Mr. and Mrs..16 E. Michigan st. (Tuesday.)
Elder John R., Mr. and Mrs...............150 New Jersey st.
Elder Edward Clinton, Mr...................150 New Jersey st.
Eldridge Geo. O., Mr. and Mrs...................24 W. 14th st.
Eldridge Edward H., Mr. and Mrs........76 E. Michigan st.
Eldridge Katherine B., Miss..76 E. Michigan st.(Tuesday.)
Eldridge Harold B., Mr......................76 E. Michigan st.
Eldridge Wm. J., Mr........................76 E. Michigan st.
Elliot Byron K., Mr. and Mrs............837 N. Meridian st.
Elliot Wm. Frederick, Mr..................837 N. Meridian st.
Elvin Wm. Higbee, Mr. and Mrs...........888 N. Illinois st.
Elvin Robert John, Mr. and Mrs...........888 N. Illinois st.
Ely James D., Mr. and Mrs..............40 W. St. Joseph st.
Emory Fred Lincoln, Mr. and Mrs..........433 N. Illinois st.
Ensley Nicholas, Mr. and Mrs............830 N. Meridian st.
Ensley Evans A., Miss....................830 N. Meridian st.
Ensley Oscar J., Mr......................830 N. Meridian st.
Ensley O. P., Mr. and Mrs................275 N. Meridian st.
Engle Willis D., Rev. and Mrs......866 N. Pennsylvania st.
English Wm. H., Mr............................Hotel English.
English Will E., Mr............................Hotel English.
Erwin Dan P., Mr. and Mrs....................The Dennison.
Erwin Helen, Miss............................The Dennison.
Erwin Hannah, Miss............................The Dennison.

Esterbrook Wm. C............134 W. Ohio st.
Esterbrook Guy R............134 W. Ohio st.
Evans Walter C., Mr............76 E. St. Joseph st.
Evans Wm. R., Mr. and Mrs............470 N. Delaware st.
Evans Edward, Mr............470 N. Delaware st.
Evans George T., Mr. and Mrs............548 N. Meridian st.
Evans Edgar H., Mr............548 N. Meridian st.
Evarts Chas. C., Dr. and Mrs............988 N. Tennessee st.

FAHNLEY Frederick, Mr. and Mrs..200 N. Meridian st.
Fahnley Carrie, Miss............200 N. Meridian st.
Fahnley Bertha, Miss............200 N. Meridian st.
Failey James F., Mr. and Mrs............585 N. Delaware st.
Failey Alice, Miss............585 N. Delaware st.
Failey Bruce, Mr............585 N. Delaware st.
Fairbanks Chas. W., Mr. and Mrs............410 Park ave.
Fairbanks Adelaide, Miss............410 Park ave.
Fanning Joseph T., Mr............The Bates House.
Farquhar Francis M., Mrs............477 N. Pennsylvania st.
Farquhar Anna, Miss............477 N. Pennsylvania st.
Farquhar Caroline H., Miss............477 N. Pennsylvania st.
Fatout Harvey Bates, Mr. and Mrs....373 N. Tennessee st.
Ferree J. C., Mr. and Mrs............630 N. Pennsylvania st.
Fesler John R., Mr. and Mrs............294 Union st.
Fesler James W., Mr............294 Union st.
Field George E., Mr. and Mrs............182 Woodruff Place.
Finch Agnes, Miss............519 N. Meridian st.
Finch Maria, Mrs............466 N. Pennsylvania st.
Finch Fabias M., Mr. and Mrs............247 Park ave.
Finch John A., Mr............247 Park ave.
Finch Alice, Miss............247 Park ave.

Fish Wm. S., Mr. and Mrs..................141 E. Pratt st.
Fish Julia, Miss..................141 E. Pratt st.
Fish Mary E., Miss..................141 E. Pratt st.
Fish Wm. Ross, Mr..................141 E. Pratt st.
Fisher Thos. G., Mr. and Mrs.................. 126 Butler st.
Fishback Wm. P., Mr. and Mrs..........733 N. Delaware st.
Fitzgerald P. H., Mr. and Mrs...........415 N. Meridian st.
Fitzgerald Laura, Miss..................415 N. Meridian st.
Ferger Charles, Mr. and Mrs.............565 N. Tennessee st.
Ferger Charles, Jr., Mr..................565 N. Tennessee st.
Ferger Carrie, Miss.........................565 N. Tennessee st.
Fitzgerald Frank, Mr..................415 N. Meridian st.
Fitzgerald Philander H., Mr..................415 N. Meridian st.
Fletcher Calvin I., Dr..................670 N. Meridian st.
Fletcher Wm. B., Dr. and Mrs..............124 N. Alabama st.
Fletcher Aileen Desmond, Miss...........124 N. Alabama st.
Fletcher Lucy Hines, Miss..................124 N. Alabama st.
Fletcher Una Cladys, Miss..................124 N. Alabama st.
Fletcher Horace H., Mr. and Mrs..............375 Home ave.
Fletcher Anna, Miss..........................859 N. Illinois st.
Fletcher Jesse, Mr..................152 N. Meridian st.
Fletcher Ruth, Miss..........................152 N. Meridian st.
    Summer residence, Millersville, Ind.
Fletcher Stephen K., Mr. and Mrs......437 N. Tennessee st.
Fletcher Stoughton J., Mr..................180 E. Ohio st.
Fletcher James L., Mrs..................810 N. Meridian st.
Fletcher Allen, Mr. and Mrs..............250 N. Meridian st.
Fletcher Mary, Miss..................250 N. Meridian st.
Fletcher James J., Mr. and Mrs............159 Christian ave.
Fletcher Frank Chase, Mr..................159 Christian ave.
Fletcher Calvin, Mr. and Mrs..................379 Home ave.

THE ELITE LIST.

Fletcher Emily, Miss.............................379 Home ave.
Fletcher Samuel H., Mr. and Mrs......344 N. Tennessee st.
Fletcher Lafayette W., Mr. and Mrs....344 N. Tennessee st.
Fletcher Chas. B., Mr. and Mrs.............370 Clifford ave.
Fletcher Stoughton A., Mr. and Mrs........352 Clifford ave.
Fletcher Emily, Miss (Teacher)................376 Home ave.
Fletcher Edward C., Mr..........................356 N. East st.
Flack Joseph F., Mr. and Mrs........1140 W. Washington st.
Flack Viola, Miss........................1140 W. Washington st.
Folsom Edwin S., Mr. and Mrs..................332 Park ave.
Folsom Mabell, Miss............................332 Park ave.
Forsyth Elijah J., Mr..........................132 Fletcher ave.
Forsyth Wm. J., Mr.............................132 Fletcher ave.
Forsyth Alice, Miss............................132 Fletcher ave.
Forsyth Elizabeth, Miss........................132 Fletcher ave.
Forsyth Clarence, Mr. and Mrs...................459 Ash St.
Forsyth Clarence, Mr. and Mrs......................Irvington.
Fortune Wm., Mr. and Mrs.............154 E. Drive, (W. P.)
Ford Eliza, Miss........................868 N. Pennsylvania st.
Ford Belle, Miss........................868 N. Pennsylvania st.
Foster Robert S., Mr. and Mrs........352 N. New Jersey st.
Foster Wallace, Mr. and Mrs..........1090 N. Tennessee st.
Foster Chas. B., Mr. and Mrs.............16 Windsor Place.
Foster Clarence M., Mr................352 N. New Jersey st.
Foster Robert S.......................352 N. New Jersey st.
Foster Rose S., Miss..................352 N. New Jersey st.
Foster Benjamin F., Mr....................410 N. Delaware st.
Foster Grace, Miss........................410 N. Delaware st.
Foster Frank S., Mr. and Mrs..............702 N. Alabama st.
Foster Edgar J., Mr. and Mrs.......339 N. Pennsylvania st.
Foster Florence Day, Miss............339 N. Pennsylvania st.

Foster Sarah W., Miss.. ....339 N. Pennsylvania st.
Foster Frances Hannon, Miss........339 N. Pennsylvania st.
Foster Chapin Clark, Mr. and Mrs...762 N. Pennsylvania st.
Foulke Wm. D. Mr........................329 E. New York st.
Francke Frederick, Mr. and Mrs..........984 N. Meridian st.
Francis Joseph P., Mr. and Mrs...........94 Woodruff Place.
Francis Louis E., Mr. and Mrs..............688 N. Illinois st.
Francis Harriet, Miss........................688 N. Illinois st.
Frank Henry, Mr. and Mrs....................644 N. Illinois st.
Frankem Isaac, Mr. and Mrs..............449 N. Tennessee st.
Fraser, Henry Scott, Mr. and Mrs..... { 754 N. Delaware st.
                                       { ....(Wednesday.)
Fraser Dwight, Mr. and Mrs...........779 E. Washington st.
Fraser Anna E., Miss....................779 E. Washington st.
Fraser Elizabeth, Miss................621 N. Pennsylvania st.
Frazer Joshua G., Mr. and Mrs.....621 N. Pennsylvania st.
Frazier Simeon, Mr. and Mrs..........................Irvington.
Frazier Elisha, Rev. and Mrs......Washington ave., Irving.
Friendly Harry Harman, Mr. and Mrs........209 Broadway.
Frenzel John P., Mr. and Mrs..................340 N. East st.
Frenzel Caroline P.............................340 N. East st.
Frenzel Oscar F..................................340 N. East st.
Frenzel Otto, Mr. and Mrs..................845 N. Illinois st.
Fugate James L., Mr. and Mrs...........825 N. Meridian st.
Fugate Fanny, Miss........................825 N. Meridian st.
Furgason John A., Mr. and Mrs........270 N. Tennessee st.
Furnas Robert M., Mr. and Mrs..............268 Central ave.

GALL Albert, Mr. and Mrs............590 N. Illinois st.
Gall Bertha, Miss....................590 N. Illinois st.
Gall Albert, Jr., Mr. and Mrs..............374 N. Illinois st.
Gall Edmund, Mr. and Mrs........... 854 N. Pennsylvania st.
Galbraith Jane, Mrs...................... ..781 N. Meridian st.
Galbraith Harriet, Miss....................781 N. Meridian st.
Galloway Clinton E., Dr. and Mrs...........444 Central ave.
Galloway Alexander, Mr. and Mrs...................27 East st.
Gallup Wm. P., Mr.........................358 N. Tennessee st.
Galvin George W., Mr. and Mrs...Downey ave., Irvington.
Galvin Mary B., Miss...................Downey ave., Irvington.
Galvin Georgia Noble.................Downey ave., Irvington.
Garber W. S., Mr. and Mrs...........784 N. Pennsylvania st.
Gardner, Ansen J., Mr. and Mrs........1028 N. Meridian st.
Gardner Fred., Mr. and Mrs......................292 Broadway.
Gaston John M., Mr. and Mrs..........147 N. New Jersey st.
Gaston Amelia Love, Miss..............147 N. New Jersey st.
Gaston Olive, Miss........................147 N. New Jersey st.
Garvin Hugh C., Mr. and Mrs..........................Irvington.
Gates Alfred D., Mr. and Mrs.............826 N. Meridian st.
Gates Edward, Mr..........................826 N. Meridian st.
Gates Frank T., Mr. and Mrs.............375 N. Tennessee st.
Gates Wm. Newkirk, Mr. and Mrs...................74 10th st.
Gavisk Francis Henry, Rev..................76 W. Georgia st.
George Jesse D., Dr. and Mrs......................367 Park ave.
Geiger George, Mr. and Mrs.....................116 E. Pratt st.
Geiger John L., Mr...............................116 E. Pratt st.
Gibney John H., Mr. and Mrs....................27 Home ave.
Gibson Mary P., Mrs......................909 N. Delaware st.
Gibson David, Mr........................ 909 N. Delaware st.

Gibson Thomas, Mrs......................284 N. Tennessee st.
Gibson Louis H., Mr. and Mrs.......830 N. Pennsylvania st.
Giles Reginald H., Mr..........................357 N. East st.
Gillette O. S. Mr. and Mrs............................Central ave.
Gillette Gertrude, Miss................................Central ave.
Gillette Frank, Mr..Central ave.
Goe M. C., Mr. and Mrs.................................Irvington.
Goe Clara, Miss..Irvington.
Golt Walter F. C., Mr. and Mrs...1024 N. Pennsylvania st.
Gooking George F., Mr. and Mrs............236 Central ave.
Goode Laban Lycurgus, Mr. and Mrs...942 N. Meridian st.
Goode Vinnie R., Miss.......................942 N. Meridian st.
Goode Charles Norton, Mr................942 N. Meridian st.
Goodwin Edwin M., Mr. and Mrs..............21 Morrison st.
Gossen Phillips, Mr. and Mrs..............870 N. Alabama st.
Gordon Irving S., Mr..............................613 N. Illinois st.
Gordon Mary, Mrs........................880 N. Pennsylvania st.
Gordon Georgia, Miss..................880 N. Pennsylvania st.
Goulding John A., Mr. and Mrs..........870 N. Alabama st.
Graff Robert, Mr. and Mrs..........................232 N. East st.
Gramling Peter, Mr. and Mrs...............500 N. Delaware st.
Graves Thos., Mr. and Mrs..............317 N. New Jersey st.
Gray Isaac P., ex-Gov.and Mrs.....661 N. Pennsylvania st.
Gray Pierce, Mr. and Mrs............. 661 N. Pennsylvania st.
Graydon Alice.................................494 N. Pennsylvania st.
Graydon Andrew, Mr. and Mrs.....494 N. Pennsylvania st.
Graydon Alexander, Mr................494 N. Pennsylvania st.
Graydon Wm. McKinney, Mr. and Mrs.....288 Central ave.
Graydon Mary M., Miss..........................288 Central ave.
Graydon Katharine, Miss........................288 Central ave.
Graydon Jean, Miss ....288 Central ave.

Graydon Douglas, Mr............................288 Central ave.
Green Hugh M., Mr. and Mrs..............857 N. Meridian st.
Greenstreet Jason H.. Mr. and Mrs...581 N. Tennessee st.
Greenstreet Flora Viola, Miss ....581 N. Tennessee st.
Greenstreet Chas. Jason, Mr...............581 N. Tennessee st.
Greer S. R., Mr....................................861 N. Illinois st.
Gregory Fred. A., Mr. and Mrs.......... 935 N. Meridian st.
Gregory Martha M., Mrs.....................935 N. Meridian st.
Griffin George O., Mr. and Mrs..........273 N. Tennessee st.
Griffin Michael S., Mr.........................273 N. Tennessee st.
Griffin George G., Mr..........................273 N. Tennessee st.
Griffin Martha B., Miss........................273 N. Tennessee st.
Griffin Brook, Miss...............................273 N. Tennessee st.
Griffith Wm. G., Mr............................307 N. Delaware st.
Griffith Theodore, Mr. and Mrs..........446 N. Tennessee st.
Griffith Elmer E., Mr. and Mrs. ....Blind Asylum.
Griffith Carl V., Mr. and Mrs..............446 N. Tennessee st.
Griffith Claude T., Mr. and Mrs..................316 Broadway.
Griffith DeWitt C., Mr. and Mrs..............701 Alabama st.
Griffith Wm. H., Mr. and Mrs............534 N. Delaware st.
Griffith John W., Mr...........................392 Bellefontaine st.
Griffith Anna, Miss..............................392 Bellefontaine st.
Griffith Martha L,...............................392 Bellefontaine st.
Griffith Pleasant H., Mr..............................357 N. East st.
Griffiths John Lewis, Mr. and Mrs.......21 Woodruff Place.
Grover Ira D., Mr. and Mrs.........................82 W. North st.
Grover Arthur B., Mr. and Mrs..................82 W. North st.
Grubb Mary, Miss............................832 N. Pennsylvania st.
Grubb Jane, Miss ....832 N. Pennsylvania st.

HACKER Thomas, Dr. and Mrs.......17 Woodruff pl.
Hackerdon Wm., Mr. and Mrs..394 N. Delaware st.
Hadley Joel W., Mr. and Mrs....................160 Park ave.
Hadley Evan, Dr. and Mrs................. 270 N. Delaware st.
Hadley Chalmers, Mr........................ 270 N. Delaware st.
Hagarth Sarah J., Mrs...............................361 Broadway.
Haines Mathias L., Rev. and Mrs...397 N. Pennsylvania st.
Haines Sam. A., Mr. and Mrs.............604 N. Alabama st.
Haines Ella E., Miss..........................604 N. Alabama st.
Haynes Jno. R , Dr. and Mrs...............264 N. Illinois st.
Hall Chas. Eli, Mr. and Mrs.........947 N. Pennsylvania st.
Hall Wm. C., Mr. and Mrs................526 N. Meridian st.
Hall Reginald H., Mrs......................210 N. Meridian st.
Hall Elisha H., Mr. and Mrs.............279 N. Tennessee st.
Hall Albert Fitch, Mr.......................279 N. Tennessee st.
Hall Geo. B., Mr. and Mrs..................275 N. Delaware st.
Hall Carrie L., Mrs...............................39 Woodruff pl.
Hall Harriet B., Mrs................................311 Park ave.
Hall Arthur F., Mr..................................311 Park ave.
Hall Emma, Miss....................................311 Park ave.
Hall Archibald M., Mr.............University ave., Irvington.
Hammel George J., Mr. and Mrs..........214 N. Alabama st.
Hammel, Wm. W., Mr......................214 N. Alabama st.
Hammel George C., Mr....................214 N. Alabama st.
Hamilton Margaret, Miss..........................160 Park ave.
Hammond Upton J., Mr. and Mrs..401 N. Pennsylvania st.
Hammond Francis J., Dr. and Mrs..790 N. Pennsylvania st.
Harden John, Rev. and Mrs..Brightwood ave., Brightwood.
Harding W. Newton, Mr. and Mrs......857 N. Alabama st.
Hanckel Henry S., Mr. and Mrs......175 N. New Jersey st.

THE ELITE LIST. 45

Hanna Henry H., Mr. and Mrs......786 N. Pennsylvania st.
Hanson Julius, Mr. and Mrs................600 N. Delaware st.
Hanson Mary, Miss............................600 N. Delaware st.
Hancock Frank, Mr............................506 N. Delaware st.
Hancock Ellen, Mrs............................506 N. Delaware st.
Harper James W., Judge and Mrs........872 N. Delaware st.
Harper Ida A., Mrs............................149 Pennsylvania st.
Hare Marcus L., Mr. and Mrs......500 N. Pennsylvania st.
Hare Clinton L., Mr. and Mrs........500 N. Pennsylvania st.
Harper Winifred, Miss......................149 Pennsylvania st.
Harper Frances A., Miss....................340 N. Meridian st.
Harris Addison C., Mr. and Mrs. { ....744 N. Meridian st.
                                 { Riverside Farm, Castlet'n
Harrison, Major, Mr. and Mrs....................78 E. Pratt st.
Harrison Benjamin F., Mr................674 N. Delaware st.
Harsein R. J., Mr............................566 N. Illinois st.
Harsein Adolph, Mr............................566 N. Illinois st.
Hartman Rebecca, Mrs..............................Central ave.
Harrison Alfred, Mrs......................252 N. Meridian st.
Harvey Delitha B............................302 N. Delaware st.
Harvey Kate P............................302 N. Delaware st.
Harvey Jessie Butler, Mrs..................302 N. Delaware st.
Haskell Wm. S , Dr. and Mrs..................331 Central ave.
Hasselman Watson, Mr. and Mrs...Central ave. and 26th st.
Hasselman Otto H., Mr. and Mrs........100 E. Michigan st.
Hasselman Miss (Thursday)..............100 E. Michigan st.
Hatch Aretus, Mr. and Mrs...................... 84 W. 2d st.
Hatherington Fred. A , Mr. and Mrs............Morton Place.
Hatfield Chas., Mr. and Mrs................191 N. New Jersey st.
Hawkins Edward, Mr. and Mrs..................324 Broadway.
Hawkins Don., Mr..................................324 Broadway.

Hawkins Roscoe, Mr. and Mrs..........376 N. Tennessee st.
Hawley Celia A..............................613 N. Illinois st.
Hays Franklin, Dr. and Mrs...................19 E. Ohio st.
Hazzard David L., Mr. and Mrs...........218 N. Alabama st.
Hazzard Frank...............................218 N. Alabama st.
Heath C. A., Mr. and Mrs...................177 Christian ave.
Heeb Emmett J., Mr. and Mrs............843 N. Delaware st.
Helm Henry, Mr. and Mrs.............621 E. Washington st.
Helm Matilda H., Miss ....621 E. Washington st.
Helm Gertrude C., Miss..................621 E. Washington st.
Helwig Frank, Mr. and Mrs................94 W. Walnut st.
Hendricks Thomas A., Mrs...............81 N. Tennessee st.
Hendricks Allan Mr.........................296 N. Meridian st.
Hendricks Ezra R., Mr......................296 N. Meridian st.
Hendricks Carolina B., Miss..............296 N. Meridian st.
Hendricks Bessie, Miss......................296 N. Meridian st.
Hendricks Laura B., Mrs....................296 N. Meridian st.
Hendricks Anna B., Miss...................611 N. Meridian st.
Hendricks Victor R., Mr. and Mrs......611 N. Meridian st.
Hendricks Eliza S...............................611 N. Meridian st.
Hendrickson Wm. A., Rev..................194 N. Illinois st.
Hendrickson Edwin A., Mr. and Mrs...297 N. Delaware st.
Hendrickson Alonzo P., Mr. and Mrs.. 800 N. Meridian st.
Henderson Wm., Mrs........................700 N. Meridian st.
Henderson John O., Mr. and Mrs..846 N. Pennsylvania st.
Henley Wm., Mr. and Mrs.....................308 College ave.
Henley Effie, Miss..............................308 College ave.
Hereth Ad., Mr. and Mrs..................256 N. Alabama st.
Hereth Lulu M., Miss......................256 N. Alabama st.
Herriott Juliet I., Mrs...........................8 Sterling st.
Herriott Wm. M., Mr..........................8 Sterling st.

THE ELITE LIST.

Herod Pirtle, Mr. and Mrs. (Thurs.)......661 N. Meridian st.
Herod Wm., Mr. and Mrs..................731 N. Meridian st.
Herod Lucy, Miss............................731 N. Meridian st.
Herod Joseph, Mr............................731 N. Meridian st.
Heron Alexander, Mr. and Mrs.............642 N. Illinois st.
Heron Mary R., Miss........................642 N. Illinois st.
Herron Frederick M., Mr. and Mrs.......700 N. Alabama st.
Herron Mary, Miss............................700 N. Alabama st.
Herron Lydia, Miss...........................700 N. Alabama st.
Herron Josephine B., Miss ....700 N. Alabama st.
Herron Fred. P................................700 N. Alabama st.
Herron Walter................................700 N. Alabama st.
Herron Katharine, Miss. ....700 N. Alabama st.
Herzsch Augustus, Mr. and Mrs ....465 Broadway.
Hetherington Fred., Mr. and Mrs..........820 N. Broadway.
Herne Catharine, Miss......cor. N. Tennessee and 11th sts.
Heywood James B., Mr. and Mrs............639 College ave.
Hicks H. S., Mr .... The Dennison.
Hicks Mary Miss............................The Dennison.
Hicks Wm. Ellen, Mr. and Mrs ...?........426 N. Illinois st.
Higgins Julius J., Mr. and Mrs.............. 242 Broadway.
Hibben Enthrakin T., Mr. and Mrs.... 648 N. Alabama st.
Hibben Harold, Mr. and Mrs..............743 N. Delaware st.
Hildebrand Phillip M., Mr. and Mrs....937 N. Meridian st.
Hildebrand Clayton S., Mr. and Mrs....277 N. Delaware st.
Hill Ralph, Mr. and Mrs..................220 E. New York st.
Hill Ralph Jr..................................220 E. New York st.
Hill Roswell S., Mr. and Mrs.....................406 Park pl.
Hill Roswell S. Jr..................................406 Park pl.
Hill Edward, Mr. and Mrs...................551 N. Illinois st.
Hilliary Ridgely B., Mr. and Mrs..........1088 N. Illinois st.

THE ELITE LIST.

Hitt Wilbur, Mr. and Mrs....................279 N. Illinois st.
Hitz Benjamin, Mr. and Mrs...........875 N. Pennsylvania st.
Hitt George C., Mr. and Mrs.............288 N. Tennessee st.
Hobbs Walton, Mr. and Mrs.........................80 Arch st.
Hobbs Wm Henry, Mr. and Mrs.........715 N. Alabama st.
Hodges Edward, Dr. and Mrs..............152 N. Meridian st.
Hollenbeck Chas. Edwin, Mr. and Mrs..........70 W. 4th st.
Hollenbeck, Jacob G., Mr. and Mrs..229 N. Pennsylvania st.
Holliday Francis T..Grand Hotel.
Holliday John, Mr. and Mrs. { ....601 Meridian st.
{ Rika Dom, Summer Home.
Holliday, John D., Mr. and Mrs................11 Morrison st.
Holliday Wm. Warren, Mr.........................11 Morrison st.
Holliday Edward J.....................................11 Morrison st.
Holloway Wm. R., Mr.................................Halcyon blk.
Holloway Cornelius B., Mr. and Mrs..........22 Home ave.
Holliday Wm., Mr. and Mrs................241 N. Meridian st.
Holliday Jacquelin, Mr........................241 N. Meridian st.
Hollowell Lynn P.................................427 N. Meridian st.
Hollowell Amos R., Mr. and Mrs..............427 College ave.
Holloway Emma J., Miss.......................988 N. Illinois st.
Hollweg Louis, Mr. and Mrs................505 N. Meridian st.
Hollweg Norma, Miss...........................505 N. Meridian st.
Holman John A., Mrs..................................44 W. North st.
Holloway Chas. E., Mr. and Mrs...844 N. Pennsylvania st.
Holmes Catherine Mrs............................76 W. Walnut st.
Holmes Ella M..76 W. Walnut st.
Holmes Rose Hanna ....76 W. Walnut st.
Holton, Dr. and Mrs............................769 N. Alabama st.
Holtzman John W......................................65 W. Market st.
Hood Frank C., Rev. and Mrs............. 63 N. Arsenal ave.

THE ELITE LIST.

Hooper Wm. D., Mr. and Mrs............469 N. Meridian st.
Hord Francis T., Mr. and Mrs........... 729 N. Delaware st.
Hord Percival C , Mr............................50 Woodruff pl.
Hord Bessie F., Miss.............................50 Woodruff pl.
Hord Mary, Miss....................................50 Woodruff pl.
Hord Wm. B., Mr...................................50 Woodruff pl.
Hord Horace, Mr...................................50 Woodruff pl.
Hord Emma B., Mrs...............................50 Woodruff pl.
Hornaday Jas. P., Mr. and Mrs............N. Pennsylvania st.
Hough Chas. E., Mr............................244 Vermont st.
Hough Emanuel, Mr. and Mrs..............244 Vermont st.
Hough Lewis G., Mr............................236 N. Illinois st.
Houston Sam L., Mr. and Mrs............584 N. Alabama st.
Hough B. F., Mrs..................................670 N. Pennsylvania st.
Hough Ida, Miss....................................670 N. Pennsylvania st.
Howland J. D., Mrs..............................627 N. Pennsylvania st.
Howland Livingston, Mrs...................340 N. Meridian st.
Howland Caroline H., Miss.............627 N. Pennsylvania st.
Howe Glenn, Mr. and Mrs..............186 N. New Jersey st.
Howley N. N., Mr..................................60 N. Alabama st.
Howland Hewitt H., Mr. and Mrs........826 N. Meridian st.
Howe Thos. C., Mr. and Mrs........................ Irvington.
Hughes Elizabeth G.............................193 Broadway.
Hunt George E., Mr....................199 N. Pennsylvania st.
Hughes Wm. A., Mr. and Mrs.....................329 Park ave.
Hughes Jessie, Miss.............................329 Park ave.
Hufford George W., Mr. and Mrs..............223 Park ave.
Humphrey Chas., Mr. and Mrs..................433 Broadway.
Humphrey M. Hervey...............................433 Broadway.
Hunt Chas. E...274 E. M chigan st.

Hubbard Willard W., Mr. and Mrs... { 309 New Jersey st. / Macatawa Park, Holland, Mich.
Hubbard Wm. H., Mr. and Mrs.............577 N. Illinois st.
Huston C. B., Mr. and Mrs.................489 N. Illinois st.
Hubbard Wm. S., Mr.........................616 N. Meridian st.
Hughes Elizabeth, Miss..................582 N. Pennsylvania st.
Husbands Wm., Mr. and Mrs....................64 Talbott ave.
Huey Milton S., Mr. and Mrs.......81 Middle Drive, (W. P.)
Huey Laura, Miss...................... 81 Middle Drive, (W. P.)
Hussey, John R., Dr. and Mrs ....30 Woodruff Place.
Hutchison Ryan, Mr. and Mrs.......... 572 N. Tennessee st.
Hunt P. G. C......................... { ....143 N. Pennsylvania st. / Winter Res., Longwood, Fla.
Hunt Ellen, Miss............................143 N. Pennsylvania st.
Hunt Georgia, Miss.......................143 N. Pennsylvania st.
Hunter Wm., Mr. and Mrs............939 N. Pennsylvania st.
Hunter Ellis F...............................939 N. Pennsylvania st.
Hubbard Kin, Mr...................................335 E. 6th st.
Hutchins Henry, Mr. and Mrs...............574 E. Market st.
Hutchinan Jacob, Mr. and Mrs........654 E. Washington st.
Hyde Nelson J., Mr. and Mrs............966 N. Tennessee st.
Hyde Nathaniel A., Rev. and Mrs. { ...... 710 Delaware st. / Fern Cottage,
Hyde Josephine, Miss .... {   Ludlow, Vir.

IDEN Thomas, Mr....................Downey ave., Irvington.
Ingersol Selma M., Miss................114 Fletcher ave.
Ingersol Henrietta, Miss.................114 Fletcher ave.
Ingersol Mary, Miss........ ....114 Fletcher ave.
Ingraham C. B., Mr. and Mrs ....265 Tennessee st.
Ingraham Mary E., Miss...............265 Tennessee st.

THE ELITE LIST.

Ingraham Lena, Miss........................265 Tennessee st.
Ingram John C., Mr. and Mrs............. ......345 Park ave.
Isensee John F., Rev. and Mrs...........228 N. California st.

JACKSON, Thos. B., Mr. and Mrs..926 N. Meridian st.
Jackson L. L., Mr...............1875 E. Washington st.
Jackson Winifred, Miss.............. 288 N. Pennsylvania st.
Jacoby Elias, Mr. and Mrs...................90 West Walnut st.
Jacobs Anna, Mrs............. 601 N. Delaware st (Tuesday.)
Jaillet Arthur D., Mr. and Mrs...........625 N. Meridian st.
Jameson Patrick H., Dr. and Mrs ....330 Broadway.
Jameson Lucy, Miss..................................330 Broadway.
Jameson Alice M., Miss ....330 Broadway.
Jameson Elizabeth K., Miss............................413 Ash st.
Jameson Betty, Miss..413 Ash st.
Jameson Ovid B., Mr. and Mrs.......737 N. Pennsylvania st.
Jameson Henry, Dr. and Mrs...............228 N. Delaware st.
Jameson Alexander, Dr. and Mrs..............22 W. North st.
Jarvis George T., Mr. and Mrs...................The Dennison.
Jenckes Joseph S., Rev. and Mrs ....1044 N. Illinois st.
Jenckes Miss.....................................1044 N. Illinois st.
Jenkins Charles, Mr. and Mrs........766 N. Pennsylvania st.
Jewar Joseph. Mr. and Mrs.......................315 Broadway.
Jillson Wm., Mr. and Mrs................739 N. Delaware st.
Johnson May, Mrs............................200 E. St. Joseph st.
Johnson Albert, Mr.....................462 N. Pennsylvania st.
Johnson Richard O., Mr. and Mrs.....cor. Wash. and State.
Johnson Sylvester, Mr. and Mrs..Central and Washington.
Johnson O. R., Mr................................The Dennison.
Johnson Alice A., Mrs........................699 N. Alabama st.

Johnson May, Miss ....699 N. Alabama st.
Johnson E. M., Mr. and Mrs..............817 N. Meridian st.
Johnston Wm. M., Mr. and Mrs..........570 N. Alabama st.
Johnston Blanche, Miss ....570 N. Alabama st.
Johnston John T., Dr. and Mrs..............388 N. Illinois st.
Johnston Samuel A., Mr. and Mrs..626 N. Pennsylvania st.
Johnston Maria, Miss...................... 517 N. Delaware st.
Johnsen Albert, Mr. and Mrs......Downey ave., Irvington.
Johnsen Gertrude, Miss..............Downey ave., Irvington.
Johnsen Emma, Miss... ....Downey ave., Irvington.
Johnsen Arthur, Mr..................Downey ave., Irvington.
Jones Mary A., Mrs.......................707 N. Alabama st.
Jones Chas., Mr. and Mrs ....78 W. 3d st.
Jones Harriet, Miss.. 78 W. 3d st.
Jones Chas. Jr., Mr................................78 W. 3d st.
Jones Lewis H, Mr. and Mrs ....442 Broadway.
Jones Benjamin, Mr. and Mrs.......785 N. Pennsylvania st.
Jones Aquilla, Mrs...........................988 N. Illinois st.
Jones Aquilla Q., Mr. and Mrs..............1053 N. Illinois st.
Jones Flora C., Mrs.....................467 N. Pennsylvania st.
Jones Eliza J., Mrs......................805 N. Meridian st.
Jones Fannie, Miss......................805 N. Meridian st.
Jordan Arthur, Mr. and Mrs.....................729 Monday st.
Jordan Railey, Mr. and Mrs.....................361 Broadway.
Julian George W., Mr............Central ave., Irvington.
Julian Paul, Mr......................Central ave., Irvington.
Judson Wm., Mr. and Mrs................ 400 N. Illinois st.
Jutt August, Mr. and Mrs............Washington, Irvington.

KAHLO, Chas., Mr. and Mrs............526 N. Illinois st.
Kahlo, George, Dr....................526 N. Illinois st.
Kahlo Henry C., Dr ....526 N. Illinois st.
Kautz Rollin F., Mr. and Mrs......Downey ave., Irvington.
Kappes Wm. Park, Mr. and Mrs.........750 N. Alabama st.
Kaufman Pearl, Miss.....................800 N. Meridian st.
Keith Ernest R., Mr. and Mrs ......826 N. Pennsylvania st.
Keller Chas. F., Mrs.....................115 Woodruff Place.
Kelsey C., Rev. and Mrs...........................84 E. Pratt st.
Kenney Edward T., Mr. and Mrs.........55 Woodruff Place.
Kenney Chas., Mr. and Mrs................222 N. Illinois st.
Kerper John Miller, Mr. and Mrs..........75 Woodruff Place.
Kerper Miss.............................75 Woodruff Place.
Kerper Mabell, Miss.....................75 Woodruff Place.
Kern Augustus B., Mr. and Mrs.........215 E. Michigan st.
Kern John W., Mr. and Mrs..........481 N. Pennsylvania st.
Ketcham Wm. A., Mr. and Mrs......................Mapleton.
Ketcham John H., Rev. and Mrs...........353 N. Illinois st.
Ketcham John L., Mr. and Mrs.........216 N. Delaware st.
Ketcham Eleanor,. Miss....................216 N. Delaware st.
Ketcham Elizabeth, Miss................216 N. Delaware st.
Ketchembach Edward, Mr. and Mrs.......Washington, Irv.
Kiefer Augustus, Mr. and Mrs............490 N. Meridian st.
Kiersted Isaac H., Mr. and Mrs......... ..126 E. Vermont st.
Kindleberger Wm. H., Dr. and Mrs.....881 N. Delaware st.
King Myron D., Mr. and Mrs.............243 N. Delaware st.
King Rebecca J., Mrs..........................188 N. Illinois st.
King Emma B., Miss...........................188 N. Illinois st.
King Roderick, Mr........ ....188 N. Illinois st.
King James W., Mr. and Mrs....................10 Seventh st.

King James W. Jr., Mr. and Mrs..............10 Seventh st.
King Robert M., Mr. and Mrs..............374 College ave.
Kingsbury J. G., Mr. and Mrs..............Irvington.
Kingsbury James L., Mr. and Mrs..Tilford ave., Irvington.
Kingsbury Edward D..............Tilford ave., Irvington.
Kinney Horace E., Mr. and Mrs..........337 N. Tennessee st.
Kipp Nathan H., Mr. and Mrs..............172 Park ave.
Kirschbaum Raphael, Mr. and Mrs..........300 N. Illinois st.
Kirschbaum May, Miss..............300 N. Illinois st.
Kitchen John M., Dr. and Mrs......145 N. Pennsylvania st.
Knapp Wallace, Mr. and Mrs.......Downey ave., Irvington.
Knefler Fred., Gen. and Mrs..............630 Washington st.
Knickerbocker David B., Rt. Rev. and Mrs..............
..............242 N. Pennsylvania st.
..............Bishopthorpe Park, Lima, Ind.
Knight Wm., Mr..............729 N. Delaware st.
Knight John R., Mr. and Mrs..............276 N. Delaware st.
Knight Louise, Miss..............276 N. Delaware st.
Knobe Bertha D., Miss..............975 N. Meridian st.
Knippenberg Henry, Mr. and Mrs..........622 N. Meridian st.
Knippenberg Miss..............622 N. Meridian st.
Kothe Wm., Mr. and Mrs..............496 E. Market st.
Koerner Conrad C., Mr. and Mrs..........951 N. Meridian st.
Koerner Carl C., Mr..............951 N. Meridian st.
Krauss Chas., Mr. and Mrs..........393 N. Pennsylvania st.
Krauss Wm. Gustave, Mr. and Mrs..391 N. Pennsylvania st.
Krauss Theodore, Mr. and Mrs......321 N. Pennsylvania st.
Kregelo Chas. E., Mr. and Mrs..............890 N. Illinois st.
Kregelo Katharine, Miss..............890 N. Illinois st.
Kuebler Carrie L., Miss..............931 N. Illinois st.
Kumler Noah W., Mr. and Mrs..........932 N. Meridian st.

THE ELITE LIST.

Kuhn Frederick, Mr. and Mrs...................300 Broadway.
Kuhn Chas. J., Mr...........................378 Broadway.
Kurtz Wm. E., Mr........................613 N. Illinois st.
Kurtz John A., Mr. and Mrs...................103 Central ave.

LAFOLLETTE Henry M., Mr............33 Whien Block.
La Follette H. W., Mr ....The Dennison.
Laird Wm. H., Mr. and Mrs..................554 N. Illinois st.
Laird Wm. H., Jr ....554 N. Illinois st.
Laird James H., Mr....................... 554 N. Illinois st.
Lamb Robert N., Mr. and Mrs ....209 Central ave.
Lamb Marietta, Miss..............................209 Central ave.
Landis Harry, Mr...... ....1011 N. Illinois st.
Landis Virginia M., Miss....................1011 N. Illinois st.
Landis Katharine D., Miss....................1011 N. Illinois st.
Landis John, Mr..............................1011 N. Illinois st.
Landon Hugh McK., Mr. and Mrs........677 N. Alabama st.
Landers Wm. F., Mr....................622 N. Pennsylvania st.
Landers Jackson, Mr. and Mrs......622 N. Pennsylvania st.
Landers Lillie B., Miss................622 N. Pennsylvania st.
Landers Franklin, Mr. and Mrs.....402 N. Pennsylvania st.
    Summer Res., Rose Lawn, Brooklyn, Ind.
Landers Julia Ethel, Miss............402 N. Pennsylvania st.
Landers Pearl, Miss....................402 N. Pennsylvania st.
Lash Hugh, Dr. and Mrs........................395 Park ave.
Latham Henry, Mr. and Mrs..............497 N. Meridian st.
Latham Wm. H., Mr. and Mrs........582 E. Washington st.
Latham Chas., Mr...... ....582 E. Washington st.
Lawrence Chas. L., Mr....................627 N. Meridian st.
Layman James T., Mr. and Mrs..................Irvington.
Layman James, Mr. and Mrs.....Central ave. and E. Wash.

Layman Elizabeth, Miss...........Central ave. and E. Wash.
Layman Thomas...................Central ave. and E. Wash.
Layman Daniel.....................Central ave. and E. Wash.
Layman James F.............................284 Lincoln ave.
Layman Louise C., Mrs .... 284 Lincoln ave.
Layman Kate, Miss ....284 Lincoln ave.
Laycock Wm. H., Mr...... ....611 N. Mississippi st.
Laycock Maude B., Miss..............622 N. Pennsylvania st.
Lazarus John S., Mr. and Mrs...........1000 N. Meridian st.
Lazarus George M., Mr.................1000 N. Meridian st.
Leathers James, Mr. and Mrs.....................Morton Place.
Leckleider John, Mr. and Mrs..............18 E. Vermont st.
Leckener Max., Mr. and Mrs...282 N. Penn. st. (Monday).
Lee Henry H., Mrs ....189 N. Illinois st.
Lee Frank W., Mr. and Mrs...............165 N. Delaware st.
Lee Fielding T., Mr. and Mrs............444 N. Tennessee st.
Lee Amanda M..200 Park ave.
Lee Anna Blanche......................................200 Park ave.
Lee Lot, Mr. and Mrs......................... ....444 Park ave.
Lefler Chas. W., Mr. and Mrs....................374 College st.
Lefler Curtis Harris...............................374 College st.
Lemon Daniel A., Mr. and Mrs..........196 N. Tennessee st.
Lemon Daisy, Miss.......................196 N. Tennessee st.
Lewis Catharine, Mrs....................528 N. Meridian st.
Lewis Catharine, Miss.................... ..528 N. Meridian st.
Lewis Chas. Allen, Mr............... ....528 N. Meridian st.
Lewis Chas. Sumner, Mr. and Mrs..........600 N. Illinois st.
Lewis Prudence E., Miss...............399 N. New Jersey st.
Leonard Helen M., Miss...............781 E. Washington st.
Levey Wm. M., Mr. and Mrs ....911 N. Delaware st.
Levey Lewis, Mr. and Mrs...................834 N. Meridian st.

THE ELITE LIST.

Lieber Otto, Mr. and Mrs..................311 N. Tennessee st.
Lieber Albert, Mr.............................558 Madison ave.
Lieber Peter, Mr. and Mrs..................558 Madison ave.
Lieber Anna, Miss . ...250 N. Alabama st.
Lieber Herman, Mr. and Mrs...............250 N. Alabama st.
Lieber Carl, Mr................................250 N. Alabama st.
Liebert Chas. L., Mr. and Mrs......853 N. Pennsylvania st.
Lilly Catharine, Mrs..........................600 N. Tennessee st.
Lilly Miss..600 N. Tennessee st.
Lilly Chas., Mr. and Mrs....................600 N. Tennessee st.
Lilly James Raynor, Mr. and Mrs....778 N. Pennsylvania st.
Lilly Josiah K., Mr. and Mrs..........675 N. Pennsylvania st.
Lilly Evan F., Mr. and Mrs................700 N. Delaware st.
Lilly James E., Mr. and Mrs...............996 N. Illinois st.
Lilly Mary, Miss...............................996 N. Illinois st.
Lilly Eli, Col. and Mrs....................454 N. Tennessee st.
Lindley John, Mrs............................The Dennison.
Lisnor David S., Mr. and Mrs.............Bates House.
Lockwood Wm. G., Mr. and Mrs..........12 Woodruff Place.
Lockwood Margaret, Miss..................12 Woodruff Place.
Long Henry Clay, Mr. and Mrs.....610 N. Pennsylvania st.
Long R. W., Dr. and Mrs...................200 N. Delaware st.
Lockhard Alvia S., Mr....................729½ N. Delaware st.
Lockhard Cordelia B., Mrs..............729½ N. Delaware st.
Lodge James, Mr. and Mrs............433 N. Pennsylvania st.
Lodge Caleb Newall, Mr ....433 N. Pennsylvania st.
Lowe John R., Mr. and Mrs.........1020 N. Pennsylvania st.
Lowe Lena Alice, Miss................1020 N. Pennsylvania st.
Lowe Winnie A............................1020 N. Pennsylvania st.
Love Nellie, Miss ....Blind Institute.
Love Mary F., Miss........................407 N. Tennessee st.

THE ELITE LIST.

Lucas Daniel R., Rev and Mrs........293 N New Jersey st.
Lucas Catharine, Miss........................293 N. New Jersey st.
Lucas Manda E..................................293 N. New Jersey st.
Luider Wm., Mr. and Mrs...................1042 N. Illinois st.
Lybrand Joseph, Mr. and Mrs....................59 Talbott ave.
Lyman Bement, Mr. and Mrs.............620 N. Tennessee st.
Lynn Wm. C., Mr. and Mrs...........................76 W. 2d st.
Lynn Chas. Jackson..76 W. 2d st.
Lyon John, Mr. and Mrs............................349 College ave.
Lyon Daisy, Miss......................................349 College ave.
Lyon Elizabeth, Miss...............................349 College ave.
Lyon Frederick, Mr..................................349 College ave.
Lyon Luther W., Mr.................................349 College ave.

McALPIN James, Mr. and Mrs..............315 Park ave.
McBride Chas. S., Mr. and Mrs..790 N. Delaware st.
McBride Frank S., Mr. and Mrs..........437 N. Delaware st.
McBride Stanley, Mr...........................437 N. Delaware st.
McCabe John P., Rev. and Mrs............271 N. Meridian st.
McCarty Nicholas, Mr......................122 N. Pennsylvania st.
McCarty Fannie J., Miss..................122 N. Pennsylvania st.
McCay Ella Bush, Mrs.........................275 N. Delaware st.
McClain M. J., Mr...................................The Dennison.
McCleary Alex. M., Mr. and Mrs............922 N. Illinois st.
McCleary Chas. A., Mr............................922 N. Illinois st.
McCleary Hill T., Mr.............................. 922 N. Illinois st.
McClung Hester, Miss................................172 N. West st.
McComb John, Rev.......................................323 Olive st.
McCormick Alfred F., Mr. and Mrs......67 Woodruff Place.
McCrea Frank, Mr. and Mrs........................357 Broadway.
McCrea Rolin Hall.......................................357 Broadway.

McCullough James, Mr. and Mrs..........985 N. Meridian st.
McCulloch David, Mr........................ 600 N. Meridian st.
McCulloch Carleton B., Mr................ 600 N. Meridian st.
McCune H. B., Mr. and Mrs.................206 Christian ave.
McCurdy George, Mr. and Mrs.......288 N. Pennsylvania st.
McCurdy Halcyone, Miss...............288 N. Pennsylvania st.
McCurdy Wm. Isaac, Mr.............288 N. Pennsylvania st.
McDonald Malcolm, Mr. and Mrs...........685 N. Illinois st.
McDonald Malcolm Scott, Mr................ 685 N. Illinois st.
McDonald J. E., Mrs..............................The Dennison.
McDonough Dewer, Mr. and Mrs..........123 E. Vermont st.
McDonough Laura, Miss.....................123 E. Vermont st.
McDougal George, Mr. and Mrs.........263 N. Tennessee st.
McDougal Chas. P., Mr....................263 N. Tennessee st.
McDowell Joseph G., Mr. and Mrs....1691 N. Meridian st.
McDowell Chas. H., Rev. and Mrs............112 Talbott ave.
McGettigan Bernard, Mr....................466 N. Meridian st.
McGettigan John E., Mr....................466 N. Meridian st.
McGilliard Martin V., Mr. and Mrs... 228 N. Tennessee st.
McGilliard Edna, Miss.....................228 N. Tennessee st.
McGregory Albert B., Mr. and Mrs......307 N. Delaware st.
McIntosh Andrew, Mr. and Mrs...........98 W. Vermont st.
McIntosh Chas. D., Mr......................98 W. Vermont st.
McIntosh Sadie E., Miss....................98 W. Vermont st.
McIntosh Eva S................................98 W. Vermont st.
McKay Horace, Mr. and Mrs....................249 Broadway.
McKay Mary, Miss............. ....249 Broadway.
McKay Cornelia, Miss............................249 Broadway.
McKee Wm. J., Mr. and Mrs............... 166 N. Meridian st.
McKee J. R., Mr. and Mrs.................674 N. Delaware st.
McKee Edward L., Mr....................673 N. Delaware st.

McKee Noble B., Mr. and Mrs......157 E. Woodruff Place.
McLain Liberty C., Mr. and Mrs.........710 N. Alabama st.
McLain Mary Ann, Miss ....597 N. Illinois st.
McMahan Sam. W., Mr. and Mrs......421 N. Delaware st.
McMaster John L., Mr. and Mrs................477 Park ave.
McMaster Edith, Miss ....477 Park ave.
McMullen W. E., Mr. and Mrs................The Dennison.
McMurray Lewis H., Mr. and Mrs......954 N. Meridian st.
McRenna John, Mr. and Mrs..............744 N. Alabama st.
McRenna Laura, Miss..........................744 N. Alabama st.
McRenzie Mary, Mrs.....................276 N. New Jersey st.
McRenzie Anna, Miss....................276 N. New Jersey st.
McQuot Eugenia, Mrs.....................512 N. Tennessee st.
McQuot Tolkerbie, Miss..................512 N. Tennessee st.
........Summer Home, Bonnie Doon, Lake Maxinkuku.
MacCurdy Wm. C., Mr. and Mrs...478 N. Pennsylvania st.
MacIntire Thos., Mr. and Mrs......762 N. Pennsylvania st.
MacIntire Mary, Miss...................762 N. Pennsylvania st.
Macbeth Frank D., Mr. and Mrs.........787 N. Alabama st.
Macbeth Edna, Miss..............................787 N. Alabama st.
Macbeth Dare, Miss..............................787 N. Alabama st.
Macintosh George L., Rev....................77 St. Joseph st.
Macy David, Mrs..................................298 N. Delaware st.
Madden Thos., Mr. and Mrs.................705 N. Illinois st.
Madden John, Mr..................................705 N. Illinois st.
Magner Jennie H., Mrs ....329 Broadway.
Maguire Albert M., Mr ....329 Broadway.
Mallendore Wm., Mr...Irvington.
Malott Volney T., Mr. and Mrs.........288 N. Delaware st.
Malott Florence M., Miss...................288 N. Delaware st.
Malott Carrie G., Miss........................288 N. Delaware st.

Malott Laura, Miss..........................288 N. Delaware st.
Malott Katharine F........................ 288 N. Delaware st.
Malott Macy, Mr. and Mrs...........851 N. Pennsylvania st.
Malpas Henry, Mr. and Mrs...............836 N. Meridian st.
Malpas Samuel, Mr..............................836 N. Meridian st.
Malpas Chas. E., Mr...... ....836 N. Meridian st.
Malock Jessie E., Miss.......................117 E. Michigan st.
Manly Ida M., Miss..22 Home ave.
Mann Henry T., Mr. and Mrs......... Ritter ave., Irvington.
Mann Wm., Capt. and Mrs................340 N. Meridian st.
Mans Frank, Mr. and Mrs......................180 N. West st.
Mansur Joseph B., Mr. and Mrs...........663 N. Meridian st.
Mansur A. B., Mrs................................10 E. Vermont st.
Mansfield Martin W., Mr. and Mrs..896 N. Illinois st.(Wed.)
Marcy W. T., Mr. and Mrs...................792 N. Meridian st.
Marmon Daniel U., Mr. and Mrs.......518 N. Delaware st.
Marmon Walter C., Mr.....................518 N. Delaware st.
Marmon Howard C., Mr....................518 N. Delaware st.
Marott Joseph, Mr. and Mrs......... ......309 E. St. Clair st.
Marott Geo. J., Mr. and Mrs...............311 E. St. Clair st.
Marott Geo. P., Mr. and Mrs.. ....478 N. Alabama st.
Martin Geo. W., Mr. and Mrs.................360 College ave.
Martin Augusta, Mrs....... ....412 Broadway.
Martin Henry, Dr. and Mrs..............169 Bellefontaine st.
Martin Louis, Mr..............................169 Bellefontaine st.
Martin Henry D., Mr... ....936 N. Illinois st.
Martin Helen, Miss............................936 N. Illinois st.
Martindale Chas., Mr. and Mrs............316 N. Meridian st.
Martindale Robert. Mr. and Mrs..................36 W. 2nd st.
Martindale E. B., Mr. and Mrs...........237 N. Meridian st.
Martindale Emma, Miss....................237 N. Meridian st.

Martindale Lynn, Mr..........................237 N. Meridian st.
Marshall Margaret, Mrs....................... ...170 Christian ave.
Mason Augustus L., Mr. and Mrs......501 N. Tennessee st.
Mason W. F., Mrs...................................The Dennison.
Matthews Claude, Gov. and Mrs........ { Hazel Bluff Farm, Clinton, Ind.
Matthews Ernest, Mr. and Mrs..............20 W. Walnut st.
Matthews Horace S., Mr.......................20 W. Walnut st.
Matthews Wilson M..............................20 W. Walnut st.
Matthews Horace T., Mr. and Mrs......980 N. Meridian st.
Mavity Chas. K., Mr. and Mrs.............862 N. Delaware st.
Maxwell Allison, Dr. and Mrs..........169 N. New Jersey st.
Maxwell Maria, Mrs........................28 Fort Wayne ave.
Maxwell Angela, Miss......................28 Fort Wayne ave.
Maxwell John M., Mr. and Mrs..........860 N. Meridian st.
Maxwell G., Mrs............................. 617 N. Meridian st.
Maxwell Marion................................617 N. Meridian st.
Maxwell Georgia, Miss......................617 N. Meridian st.
Mayer Chas., Mr. and Mrs.................776 N. Meridian st.
Mayer Ferd., Mr. and Mrs.................584 N. Delaware st.
Mayo Abbie, Mrs..........................562 N. Pennsylvania st.
Mayo Lucy, Miss..........................552 N. Pennsylvania st.
Mayo Henrietta, Miss................. 562 N. Pennsylvania st.
Mayo Anna, Miss........................562 N. Pennsylvsnia st.
Mayo Sadie, Miss.......................562 N. Pennsylvania st.
Medearis Chas. Wm., Mr..............462 N. Pennsylvania st.
Medearis Fletcher C., Mr...... ......462 N. Pennsylvania st.
Meigs Lura, Miss ....409 N. Pennsylvania st.
Meigs Mary, Miss......................409 N. Pennsylvania st.
Mendenhall Johnson, Mr. and Mrs..........859 N. Illinois st.
Merrill, Miss......... ....257 N. Tennessee st.
Merrill Katherine, Miss..........227 N. Tennessee st. (Wed.)

Meyer August, Mr. and Mrs......................131 Home ave.
Meyer Chas. F., Mr. and Mrs..............323 N. Delaware st.
Messick John F., Mr. and Mrs...............159 Woodruff pl.
Michie Albert, Mr. and Mrs................656 N. Alabama st.
Milburn Joseph A., Rev. and Mrs...........32 E. Vermont st.
Miller Hugh T. H...Irvington.
Miller Samuel, Mr. and Mrs................665 N Delaware st.
Miller Wm. H., Mr. and Mrs... ....665 N. Delaware st.
Miller Jessie, Miss............................665 N. Delaware st.
Miller Frank, Mr. and Mrs... ....Highland Home.
Miller Valette, Miss.................................Highland Home.
Miller Winifred, Mr. and Mrs.......759 N. Pennsylvania ave.
Miller Enrique C., Mr. and Mrs...........580 N. Delaware st.
Millard Chas. S., Mr. and Mrs.............655 N. Delaware st.
Milligan Harvey J., Mr. and Mrs..........735 N. Delaware st.
Milliken Lynn, Mr. and Mrs....1134 N. Meridian st.(Tues.)
Minor Benj. B., Mr. and Mrs...............956 N. Meridian st.
Minor Eugene V., Mrs..........................956 N. Meridian st.
Minor Gertrude, Miss........................ 956 N. Meridian st.
Mitchell George G., Rev. and Mrs.........400 N. Illinois st.
Mitchell Florence C., Miss.....................400 N. Illinois st.
Moffett Edward, Dr...... ....860 N. Meridian st.
Moore John, Mr. and Mrs..................519 N. Meridian st.
Moore Arthur C., Mr...... ... .519 N. Meridian st.
Moore Deborah, Mrs..........................75 E. St. Joseph st.
Moore Thos. Claxton, Mr...................75 E. St. Joseph st.
Moore Miriam, Miss..........................75 E. St. Joseph st.
Moore Louise Duane...... ....75 E. St. Joseph st.
Moore Scott, Mr. and Mrs........................24 Walnut st.
Moore Ella, Miss.......................................24 Walnut st.
Moore Mary S., Mrs.. ......786 N. Pennsylvania st. (Tues.)

THE ELITE LIST.

Moore Julia, Miss..........................786 N. Pennsylvania st.
Moore Deborah, Miss....................786 N. Pennsylvania st.
Moore John L., Mr. and Mrs...........372 N. East st.
Moore Lillian, Miss...........................372 N. East st.
Moore Agnes, Miss..........................493 Meridian st.
Moorehead Thos., Mr. and Mrs.......928 N. Meridian st.
Moorehead Robert, Mr....................928 N. Meridian st.
Moorehead Maude, Miss.................928 N. Meridian st.
Moores Charles, Mr........................232 N. Alabama st.
Moores Julia, Mrs...........................232 N. Alabama st.
Moores Janet, Miss.........................232 N. Alabama st.
Moores Merrill, Mr..........................232 N. Alabama st.
Morris Kate Perry, Mrs...................667 N. Delaware st.
Morris N., Mrs................................275 N. Meridian st.
Morris Kittie, Miss...........................275 N. Meridian st.
Morris Thos. A., Mr.........................100 Central ave.
Morris John I., Mr...........................100 Central ave.
Morris Thos. O'Neil, Mr. and Mrs......52 Central ave.
Morris Chester, Mr...........................52 Central ave.
Morris Edward B., Mr. and Mrs......317 N. Delaware st.
Morris John D., Mr. and Mrs..........103 Woodruff pl.
Morris Jas. W., Mr. and Mrs...........247 N. Meridian st.
Morrison Wm. Harper, Mr. and Mrs.199 N. Pennsylvania st.
Morrison Frank W., Mr..................466 N. Pennsylvania st.
Morrison Anna B., Mrs..................621 N. Tennessee st.
Morrison F. W., Mrs.......................187 N. Pennsylvania st.
Morrell Lewis Herbert, Mr. and Mrs......292 N. Illinois st.
Morrow Wilson, Judge and Mrs..........358 N. Meridian st.
Morrow Nathaniel F., Mr and Mrs........222 N. Illinois st.
Morse Samuel E., Mr. and Mrs.............292 N. Illinois st.
Mueller George J., Mr. and Mrs............137 Central ave.

THE ELITE LIST.

Mullen Wm. F., Mr. and Mrs..............481 Mississippi st.
Murdock Thos. J., Mr..............826 N. Meridian st.
Murphy John W., Mr. and Mrs. (Tues.)..............
..............239 N. Pennsylvania st.
Murphy John H., Mr. and Mrs..............117 E. Michigan st.
Murphy Harry, Mr. and Mrs..............374 Park ave.
Mustard Mary V., Mrs..............Blind Asylum.
Mutchner Philip, Mr. and Mrs..............377 Broadway.
Myers W. R., Mr..............The Dennison.

NARDYKE Addison, Mr. and Mrs..605 N. Delaware st.
Nardyke Chas. E., Mr..............605 N. Delaware st.
Nardyke Walter A., Mr..............605 N. Delaware st.
Nash Laura Barney, Mrs..............180 E. Drive. (W. P.)
Nay Dewitt, Mr. and Mrs..............381 N. Tennessee st.
New Frank R., Mr. and Mrs..............426 N. Illinois st.
New Geo. W., Mrs..............143 N. Michigan st.
New Helen Miss..............143 N. Michigan st.
New Dudley J., Mr..............143 N. Michigan st.
New Harry Stewart, Mr. and Mrs..............476 N. Tennessee st.
New John C., Hon. and Mrs..............272 N. Pennsylvania st.
New Elizabeth R., Miss..............272 N. Pennsylvania st.
Newcomb Horatio, Mr. and Mrs..............275 N. Pennsylvania st.
Newcomb Eliza P., Mrs..............21 Morrison st.
Newcomer F. S., Mrs..............886 N. Pennsylvania st.
Newcomer, Miss..............886 N. Pennsylvania st.
Nichol Willard, Mrs..............277 N. Delaware st.
Nicholas Anna, Miss..............20 E. Pratt st.
Nicholi Chas. A., Mr. and Mrs..............598 Park ave.
Nichols Edwin, Mr. and Mrs..............519 N. Pennsylvania st.
Nichols Benj. O., Mr..............519 N. Pennsylvania st.

Nicholson Meredith..........................1087 N. Tennessee st.
Nicholson Willis, Mrs.........................1087 N. Tennessee st.
Nicholson Valentine, Mr. and Mrs..............248 Broadway.
Nicholson, Miss...............................248 Broadway.
Nicholson Mary, Miss..........................248 Broadway.
Niblack Wm. E., Mrs ....77 West N. st.
Niblack Eliza, Miss ....77 West N. st.
Niblack Sarah, Miss...........................77 West N. st.
Noble Wm. T., Mr. and Mrs.....................858 N. Meridian st.
Noble Harriet, Miss.......................Ritter ave., Irvington.
Noble Lazarus Mr..........................Ritter ave., Irvington.
Norton Pierce, Mr. and Mrs...................321 Broadway.
Nowell Frank, Mr. and Mrs...................308 N. Delaware st.

O'CONNOR M., Mr. and Mrs..................32 Central ave.
O'Connor Joseph S., Mr....................32 Central ave.
O'Connor Edward J.........................32 Central ave.
O'Connor Wm. L., Mr. and Mrs..............204 Christian ave.
Ogle Earl, Mr. and Mrs....................400 N. Meridian st.
Ogle Alfred, Mr. and Mrs ....755 N. Pennsylvania st.
Ogle Albert A., Rev. and Mrs..............266 N. Alabama st.
Ogle Robert C., Mr........................266 N. Alabama st.
Ohr John H., Mr. and Mrs..................448 N. Meridian st.
Ohr Martin Taylor, Mr. and Mrs............20 E. Pratt st.
Oliver John H., Dr. and Mrs...............134 N. Illinois st.
O'Reilly E. J., Mr. and Mrs...............705 N. Illinois st.
O'Reilly A. J., Mr........................The Dennison.
Osborn Elisha, Mr. and Mrs ....753 New Jersey st.
Osgood Mason J., Mr. and Mrs..............627 N. Meridian st.
Ostermeyer Fred., Mr. and Mrs ....592 E. Market st.
Ostermeyer Mollie J., Miss................592 E. Market st.

THE ELITE LIST. 67

Ostermeyer Fred., Mr. and Mrs......722 E. Washington st.
Overman Wm. B., Mr. and Mrs ....382 N. Meridian st.
Oxenford John, Mr. and Mrs..201 N. Pennsylvania st.(Wed.)

PADDOCK Elizabeth, Mrs......Downey ave., Irvington.
Paddock Mary, Miss..........Downey ave., Irvington.
Painter Herbert Brown, Mr................10 E. Vermont st.
Pantzer Hugo, Dr. and Mrs..................194 E. Michigan st.
Parmellee David, Mr. and Mrs......229 N. Pennsylvania st.
Parker H. C., Mr..The Dennison.
Parrott Ellsworth, Mr. and Mrs ....682 N. Alabama st.
Parry Thos. H., Mr. and Mrs ....1015 N. Illinois st.
Parry David M., Mr. and Mrs ....1104 N. Tennessee st.
Patterson John P., Mr....... ....8 Woodruff Place.
Patterson Mary, Miss................................19 E. Ohio st.
Patterson Jennie, Mrs ....298 N. Delaware st.
Pattison Sarah J., Mrs........................512 N. Illinois st.
Pattison Day C., Mr..............................512 N. Illinois st.
Pattison Samuel L., Mr.......................512 N. Illinois st.
Pattison Wm. A., Mr. and Mrs...... ....640 N. Illinois st.
Paver John M., Mr. and Mrs ....453 Park ave.
Paver Augusta, Miss...............................453 Park ave.
Paver John, Mr ....453 Park ave.
Payne Frank C., Mr. and Mrs.... 1091 N. Pennsylvania st.
Payne LeGrand H., Mr. and Mrs..........54 Woodruff Place.
Pearce Chas., Mr. and Mrs...................374 N. Illinois st.
Pearce C. W., Mr ....374 N. Illinois st.
Pearson Chas., Mr. and Mrs..............38 N. St. Joseph st.
Pearson John R., Mr. and Mrs......578 N. Pennsylvania st.
Peck Thos., Mr. and Mrs........................78 10th st. W.
Peck Edwin C., Mr ....78 10th st. W.

THE ELITE LIST.

Peck Benjamin B., Mr. and Mrs. (Monday)..............
..............................651 N. Pennsylvania st.
Peele Wm. A., Jr., Mr. and Mrs........277 E. New York st.
Pence Carrie Coburn, Mrs...................................Ash st.
Perkins Elliot S., Mr. and Mrs.......425 N. Pennsylvania st.
Perrot Peter H......................82 W. New York st.
Perry Oran, Mr. and Mrs....................725 N. Delaware st.
Perry John Calvin, Mr. and Mrs..........667 N. Delaware st.
Perry Arba Thomas, Mr.....................667 N. Delaware st.
Perry Chas. C., Mr. and Mrs..................724 N. Illinois st.
Phillips C. S., Mr..............471 N. Pennsylvania st.
Phillips Grace, Miss..............471 N. Pennsylvania st.
Phillips Kate, Miss..............471 N. Pennsylvania st.
Phillips Samuel, Mr. and Mrs..................246 Central ave.
Piel Wm. T......................645 E. Washington st.
Piel Mary, Miss..................645 E. Washington st.
Piel Henry Wm., Mr. and Mrs........700 E. Washington st.
Piel Chas. Frederick, Mr. and Mrs....706 E. Washington st.
Pierce Robert B. F., Mr. and Mrs........654 N. Meridian st.
Pierce Edward, Mr......................654 N. Meridian st.
Pierce Henry D., Mr. and Mrs..............725 N. Meridian st.
Pierce Elizabeth, Miss. ....725 N. Meridian st.
Pierson Cheron, Mr. and Mrs..................... 22 W. 14th st.
Pierson John C., Mr. and Mrs............1108 N. Meridian st.
Pierson Ernst, Mr......................1108 N. Meridian st.
Piercy J. Wilbur, Mr. and Mrs...............724 N. Illinois st.
Pink Herman, Dr. Mrs......................103 N. Meridian st.
Platter Amelia W., Miss.................247 N. Meridian st.
Potter Wm. Henry, Mr. and Mrs.........596 N. Alabama st.
Potter Lilian P., Miss...................596 N. Alabama st.
Potter Theo., Dr. and Mrs..............504 N. New Jersey st.

Potts Lizzie, Mrs..................................39 Woodruff pl.
Potts Edward G., Mr...........................39 Woodruff pl.
Potts Alfred F., Mr. and Mrs...35 Woodruff pl. (Thursday)
Porter Edward B., Mr. and Mrs..........124 E. Michigan st.
Porter Geo. I., Mr.....................................The Dennison.
Porter Albert G., Hon....................501 N. Tennessee st.
Porter Harriet, Miss......................284 N. Pennsylvania st.
Porter Henry C..The Dennison.
Porter George T...................................... The Dennison.
Powell George W .... 395 Broadway.
Powell Fred. D...395 Broadway.
Powell Elizabeth J., Mrs........Central and Washington sts.
Pratt J. F., Mrs. ....569 N. Pennsylvania st. (Friday)
Pratt Julius T., Mr. and Mrs........569 N. Pennsylvania st.
Praigg David T., Mr. and Mrs............915 N. Delaware st.
Pray Samuel D., Mr. and Mrs..............1063 N. Illinois st.
Price John J., Mr. and Mrs....739 N. Alabama st. (Monday)
Pullis Eliza A., Mrs......................626 N. Pennsylvania st.
Pyle Anna, Miss...............................492 College st.

RABB Albert, Mr. and Mrs...............24 Christian ave.
Rafert Christopher T., Mr. and Mrs...603 N. Del. st.
Rafert Jennie, Miss...... ....603 N. Delaware st.
Railsback Chas., Mr. and Mrs.............846 N. Illinois st.
Ramsey Leah P., Mrs.......................260 N. Illinois st.
Rand Frederick, Judge......... ....270 N. Illinois st.
Randall Theo. A., Mr. and Mrs...........73 E. St. Joseph st.
Randolph Geo. R., Mr. and Mrs.........832 N. Meridian st.
Randolph W. R., Mr......................832 N. Meridian st.
Randolph Parker, Mr......................832 N. Meridian st.
Ranger John H., Rev. and Mrs...........12 E. Michigan st.

Rankin Agnes E., Miss ... 958 N. Alabama st.
Rankin Louise, Miss ... 958 N. Alabama st.
Raschig Geo. L., Mr ... 247 N. Tennessee st.
Raschig Louise, Miss ... 1038 N. Illinois st.
Raschig Florence, Miss ... 1038 N. Illinois st.
Raschig Charles, Mr ... 1038 N. Illinois st.
Raschig George, Mr. and Mrs ... 59 Woodruff Place.
Raschig Maurice H., Mr ... 260 N. Illinois st.
Ratliff Russell ... Blind Asylum.
Ray Elizabeth, Miss ... 275 N. Pennsylvania st.
Ray Lucia Holliday, Miss ... 275 N. Pennsylvania st.
Ray John W., Col. and Mrs ... 275 N. Pennsylvania st.
Ray Frank E., Dr ... Insane Hospital.
Raymond Perley B., Mr. and Mrs ... 45 Woodruff Place.
Raymond Henry, Mr ... 45 Woodruff Place.
Reagan Amos, Mr. and Mrs ... 445 Central ave.
Ream Laura, Miss ... 600 N. Alabama st.
Recker Gustave, Mr. and Mrs ... 952 N. Meridian st.
Redman Wm. M., Mr. and Mrs ... Ritter ave., Irvington.
Reed Wilson, Dr. and Mrs ... 794 E. Washington st.
Reed Wilson H., Mr ... 794 E. Washington st.
Reed Edward H., Mr ... 794 E. Washington st.
Reed Sadie E., Miss ... 401 N. East st.
Rees Robert H. Mr. and Mrs ... 650 N. Alabama st.
Rees Ruby Almeda, Miss ... 650 N. Alabama st.
Reese Ferdinandina, Mrs ... 615 N. Pennsylvania st.
Reese Lillie, Miss ... 615 N. Pennsylvania st.
Reese Louis Charles, Mr ... 615 N. Pennsylvania st.
Reeves Edward, Mr ... 420 N. Delaware st.
Reeves Miss ... 420 N. Delaware st.
Reeves Lillian, Miss ... 420 N. Delaware st.

THE ELITE LIST. 71

Reeves Richard Demsey, Mr. and Mrs..517 N. Delaware st.
Reeves Sarah, Mrs..........................517 N. Delaware st.
Reeves Richard R., Mr. and Mrs............863 N. Illinois st.
Reeves Richard E., Mr....................863 N. Illinois st.
Reid Samuel, Mr. and Mrs................675 N. Alabama st.
Reinberlin Albert C., Dr. and Mrs..............298 Park ave.
Reinhard George L., Judge and Mrs...1024 N. Meridian st.
Reinhard Anna, Miss......................1024 N. Meridian st.
Reynolds Frank, Mr. and Mrs..............15 West North st.
Reynolds May, Miss..........................15 West North st.
Reynolds Elizabeth, Miss....................15 West North st.
Reynolds Ada A., Miss......................15 West North st.
Rexford Edwin Eugene, Mr. and Mrs.....848 N. Illinois st.
Rhodes Sam. S., Mr. and Mrs..............766 N. Alabama st.
Rhodes Clarence R., Mr....................766 N. Alabama st.
Rhodes Wm. A., Mr. and Mrs............444 N. Meridian st.
Richards Wm. A., Maj. and Mrs...975 N. Pennsylvania st.
Richards Hugh R., Mr................975 N. Pennsylvania st.
Richards E. N., Mr. and Mrs........453 N. Pennsylvania st.
Richards Nellie, Miss................453 N. Pennsylvania st.
Richardson Sara, Mrs......................168 N. Meridian st.
Richie Hunter, Mr. and Mrs..........Downey ave., Irvington.
Ridenour Martha, Mrs.................864 N. Pennsylvania st.
Ridenour Emma B......................864 N. Pennsylvania st.
Ridgely Henry D., Mr. and Mrs..............71 E. Seventh st.
Riley James Whitcomb, Mr....................The Dennison.
Rink Joseph, Mr. and Mrs................958 N. Meridian st.
Ritter Eli, Mr. and Mrs........................208 Central ave.
Ritter Halstead T., Mr........................208 Central ave.
Ritter Caroline, Mrs.................... Washington, Irvington.
Ritter Harriet, Miss....................Washington, Irvington.

Ritter Frederick......................Washington, Irvington.
Ritter Caroossa......................Washington, Irvington.
Roache Addison L., Mr. and Mrs...593 N. Pennsylvania st.
Roache Belle W., Miss..............593 N. Pennsylvania st.
Roache, Jamie E....................593 N. Pennsylvania st.
Robbins Erwin, Mr. and Mrs..............12 W. North st.
Robbins Earl G., Mr....................12 W. North st.
Robbins Sarah Ann, Mrs..................12 W. North st.
Robbins Chas. F., Mr. and Mrs....248 N. Penn. st.(Thurs.)
Robbins Corinna E., Miss............466 N. Pennsylvania st.
Roberts, Mr. and Mrs....................570 N. Meridian st.
Roberts John, Mr. and Mrs...................Quella Farm.
Roberts Mary M., Miss.......................Quella Farm.
Robertson James E., Mr. and Mrs........177 N. Alabama st.
Robertson Alexander M., Mr. and Mrs.480 N. Meridian st.
Robinson Edward J., Mr. and Mrs..953 N. Pennsylvania st.
Robinson Louise O., Mrs......................341 Broadway.
Robinson Wilbur S., Dr......................341 Broadway.
Robinson Louise Jenkins, Miss...............341 Broadway.
Robinson Josephine.........................84 E. Michigan st.
Robinson Kate, Miss........................251 N. Meridian st.
Robinson Elizabeth Yandis, Mrs..........84 E. Michigan st.
Robinson Joseph R., Mr....................84 E. Michigan st.
Robinson Samuel S., Mr. and Mrs...........The Deninson.
Robison Russell D., Mr.................303 N. New Jersey st.
Robson John, Mr. and Mrs..................73 E. Walnut st.
Rogers Newall, Mr.........................952 N. Meridian st.
Rogers James W., Mr. and Mrs............952 N. Meridian st.
Roll Wm. H., Mr. and Mrs.............475 N. Pennsylvania st.
Roll, Edward P. Mr...................475 N. Pennsylvania st.
Rollins Sylvester A......................77 Highland ave.

Roney Henry Clay, Mr. and Mrs.................422 Park ave.
Roney Chas. S., Mr. and Mrs..................298 Park ave.
Root Annie E., Mrs..........................566 N. Delaware st.
Root Oliver H., Mr. and Mrs.........647 N. Pennsylvania st.
Root Fannie, Miss.................... ......647 N. Pennsylvania st.
Rose F. W., Dr. and Mrs...... ....815 N. Meridian st.
Ross Morris, Mr. and Mrs......98 W. Walnut st. (Tuesday).
Roundthaler J. A., Rev. and Mrs........
....994 N. Meridian st.   Lake
Roundthaler Marion, Miss 994 N. Meridian st. } Maxinkuckee
Roundthaler Ethiel, Miss.994 N. Meridian st.   Ind.
Roundthaler Robert, Mr..994 N. Meridian st.
Rowl Louis M., Dr. and Mrs...... ....134 N. Meridian st.
Ruckle Nicholas R., Mr. and Mrs.........1057 N. Illinois st.
Rufus Edwin, Dr and Mrs................257 N. Delaware st.
Rufus Lewis, Mr........................257 N. Delaware st.
Runnels O. S., Dr. and Mrs................ 600 N. Meridian st.
Runnels Sollis, Dr. and Mrs..............258 N. Tennessee st.
Ruschaupt Catherine E., Mrs........640 N. Pennsylvania st.
Russell George W., Mr. and Mrs......................Irvington.
Ryan James B., Mr. and Mrs...........290 N. New Jersey st.

*S*ARGENT C. S., Rev and Mrs.........270 Central ave.
Sargent James F. T., Mr..............270 Central ave.
Sayles Charles F., Mr. and Mrs...........712 N. Delaware st.
Scharff Nathan, Mr. and Mrs..................433 N. Illinois st.
Schepard Silas, Mr. and Mrs...............772 N. Alabama st.
Schepard Frank, Mr.........................772 N. Alabama st.
Schepard Silas, Jr..........................772 N. Alabama st.
Schepard Harriet A........................772 N. Alabama st.
Schellschmidt Conrad, Mr. and Mrs..855½ N. New Jersey st.

Schellschmidt Adolph, Mr..........................246 E. Ohio st.
Schellschmidt Emma, Miss........................246 E. Ohio st.
Schleicher Adolph, Mr. and Mrs.............998 Mississippi st.
Schliewen Richard, Mr. and Mrs........545 N. Tennessee st.
Schmidt Lorenz, Mr. and Mrs...........162 N. New Jersey st.
Schmidt John W., Mr. and Mrs............740 N. Delaware st.
Schmidt Oscar W., Mr..........................373 N. Delaware st.
Schmidt Elizabeth M., Mrs...................373 N. Delaware st.
Schmidt Edward H., Mr........................373 N. Delaware st.
Schmidt Wm. H., Mr..............................373 N. Delaware st.
Schnull Henry, Mr. and Mrs......................165 Central ave.
Schnull Gustav, Mr. and Mrs.....................285 N. Illinois st.
Schoppenhorst Wm. H., Mr. and Mrs..........317 College st.
Schrader Louise, Miss...Marlowe blk.
Schurman Henry, Mr. and Mrs........575 N. Pennsylvania st.
Schurman Chas., Mr. and Mrs..............78 W. Michigan st.
Schurman Edward, Mr. and Mrs..................The Dennison.
Schwinge Henry, Mr. and Mrs.......................168 Park ave.
Scott Ida, Miss..384 W. North St.
Scott John E., Mr. and Mrs ....677 N. Illinois st.
Scott Thomas D., Mr. and Mrs.................376 N. Illinois st.
Scott Jane, Miss..376 N. Illinois st.
Scott Ray, Miss..376 N. Illinois st.
Scott Adam, Mr. and Mrs.....................136 W. Maryland st.
Scott Wm., Mr. and Mrs.........................503 N. Delaware st.
Sears Oscar Wilson, Mrs......................277 N. Delaware st.
Seaton Wm. D., Mr. and Mrs.........................235 Park ave.
Seaton Helen, Miss..235 Park ave.
Seaton Wm., Mr..235 Park ave.
Seaton Albert, Mr...235 Park ave.
Seaton Howland, Mr......................................235 Park ave.

Seaton Clark, Mr......................................235 Park ave.
Seeds Russell McClellan, Mr. and Mrs..181 E. Drive (W.P.)
Sells Michael, Mr. and Mrs................321 N. New Jersey st.
Sells Corwin..321 N. New Jersey st.
Selleck Rhoda E., Miss...................................86 E. Pratt st.
Serfert W. L., Mr...................................The Dennison.
Severin Henry, Mr. and Mrs..................573 N. Meridian st.
Sequin Edward S., Mr. and Mrs..................383 Park ave.
Sequin Henry..383 Park ave.
Sewall Elmer C., Mr. and Mrs............373 N. Tennessee st.
Sewall Alice M., Miss.............................373 N. Tennessee st.
Sewall Theodore Lovett. Mr..........343 N. Pennsylvania st.
Sewall May Wright, Mrs. ....343 N. Pennsylvania st.
Seymour George F., Mr. and Mrs.........601 N. Delaware st.
Share George R., Mr. and Mrs............366 N. Tennessee st.
Share Louis Adsit..................................366 N. Tennessee st.
Share Mary Frances.........................366 N. Tennessee st.
Shank Wm. H., Mr. and Mrs..................................Irvington.
Shank Clara, Miss...Irvington.
Shank Florence, Miss...Irvington.
Shank Samuel, Mr..Irvington.
Sharpe Thos. Mrs.........................850 Pennsylvania ave.
Sharpe Belle, Miss........................850 Pennsylvania ave.
Sharpe Joseph K., Mrs..........................670 N. Illinois st.
Sharpe Julia G., Miss..............................670 N. Illinois st.
Sharpe Anna T., Miss..........................670 N. Illinois st.
Sharpe Joseph K., Jr., Mr. and Mrs..............................
.................................640 N. Delaware st. (Tuesday).
Shaver James E., Mr. and Mrs................45 N. Illinois st.
Shaver Miss..45 N. Illinois st.
Shaw John M., Mr. and Mrs..................268 Park ave.

THE ELITE LIST.

Shaw Phillip J., Mr. and Mrs...................248 N. East st
Shedd Susan, Mrs......................................11 Woodruff pl.
Shedd Edwin H.. Mr..................................11 Woodruff pl.
Shepard Frederick K., Mr. and Mrs..........13 Woodruff pl.
Sherrill Frank A., Mr. and Mrs................32 W. St. Joseph st.
Shiel R. R., Mr. and Mrs...........................551 N. Meridian st.
Shipp Joseph P., Mr. ....540 N. Delaware st.
Shipp Miss........................540 N. Delaware st. (Tuesday).
Shoemaker J. C., Mr. and Mrs.................923 N. Illinois st.
Shoemaker John C....................................923 N. Illinois st.
Sickles Fred., Mr. and Mrs........................272 Walnut st.
Sickels Wm. W , Rev. and Mrs................351 N. East st.
Sickels Catherine, Miss.............................351 N. East st.
Sickels Lucia H...351 N. East st.
Sickels Henry C., Mr. and Mrs............. 1083 N. Illinois st.
Sidener James B.......................................443 Broadway.
Siefert Frances, Mrs..The Dennison.
Silvester Wm. R., Mr. and Mrs......597 N. Pennsylvania st.
Silvester Wm. B., Mr.........................597 N. Pennsylvania st.
Simmonds Fernandez, Mr. and Mrs.....629 N. Meridian st.
Simmonds Nellie E., Miss..................629 N. Meridian st.
Simmonds Blanche A., Miss............... 629 N. Meridian st.
Sinclair Robert S., Mr.........................122 W. Michigan st.
Sinnott Nicholas, Mr. and Mrs...............245 Central ave.
Smith Wm. C., Mr. and Mrs ....410 N. Pennsylvania st.
Smith Anna T ....410 N. Pennsylvania st.
Smith Horace, Mr. and Mrs............578 N. Pennsylvania st.
Smith Ed. S., Rev. and Mrs....................595 E. 11th st.
Smith Francis, Mr. and Mrs.............622 N. Tennessee st.
Smith Ethel, Miss..............................622 N. Tennessee st.
Smith Frances, Miss..........................622 N. Tennessee st.

Smith Chas. W., Mr. and Mrs....................79 E. Pratt st.
Smith Grace, Miss..................................79 E. Pratt st.
Smith Margaret E....................................79 E. Pratt st.
Smith Albert P.......................................79 E. Pratt st.
Smith John E., Mr. and Mrs....................118 E. Pratt st.
Smith Harold O., Mr..............................118 E. Pratt st.
Smith Kate May, Miss............................118 E. Pratt st.
Smith Josephine, Miss............................118 E. Pratt st.
Smith Joshua S., Mr. and Mrs............351 N. Tennessee st.
Smith Jeanette, Miss..........................351 N. Tennessee st.
Smith Alonzo G., Mr. and Mrs............264 N. Tennessee st.
Smith Theresa H., Mrs............................23 Home ave.
Smith Goldwin J., Mr..............................23 Home ave.
Smith Gail, Miss....................................23 Home ave.
Smith A. Judson, Mr. and Mrs............139 W. Michigan st.
Smith Chas. W., Mr. and Mrs..................340 College st.
Smith Jennie, Miss................................340 College st.
Smith John W., Mr. and Mrs..............366 N. Alabama st.
Smith C. F., Mr. and Mrs.........................The Dennison.
Smythe Wm. H., Mr. and Mrs..........1089 N. Tennessee st.
Snider Geo. W., Mr. and Mrs............785 N. Delaware st.
Snow Alpheus, Mr. and Mrs..............536 N. Delaware st.
Snyder David E., Mr. and Mrs..................27 Home ave.
Snyder Alice May, Miss...........................27 Home ave.
Socwell Sam. Henry, Mr. and Mrs......228 N. Alabama st.
Somerville James, Mr. and Mrs..........378 N. Meridian st.
Somerville Alfred H.............................378 N. Meridian st.
Somerville James.................................378 N. Meridian st.
Somerville Alice, Miss.........................378 N. Meridian st.
Somerville John Murray, Mr...............378 N. Meridian st.
Southern Jacob T., Mr. and Mrs.......553 N. Tennessee st.

Speare Henry N., Mr. and Mrs..........800 N. Tennessee st.
Spades Michael H., Mr. and Mrs...Windsor pk., Illinois st.
Spann John, Mr. and Mrs .... 199 Broadway.
Spann John S., Mr. and Mrs..........163 N. Pennsylvania st.
Spann Henry, Mr......................163 N. Pennsylvania st.
Spann Thos. H., Mr. and Mrs.............502 N. Delaware st.
Spann Anna, Miss......................502 N. Delaware st.
Sperry Harriet Lavina, Mrs........................291 Park ave.
Sprague M. G., Miss....................248 N. Pennsylvania st.
Sproule M. F., Mrs.................345 N. Pennsylvania st.
Sproule Anna, Miss..................... 345 N. Pennsylvania st.
Spruance Alexander, Mr. and Mrs...954 N. Pennsylvania st.
Staats Louise, Mrs.......................424 N. New Jersey st.
Staats Margaret, Mrs.......................10 E. Michigan st.
Staats T. Martin, Mrs.......................10 E. Michigan st.
Stackhouse Urbine, Dr. and Mrs...776 N. Pennsylvania st.
Stafford Earle E., Mr................................Grand Hotel.
Stalnaker Frank D., Mr. and Mrs..........1055 N. Illinois st.
Stanton Howard M..................... ......523 N. Delaware st.
Stanton Ambrose P., Mr. and Mrs.......523 N. Delaware st.
Stanton Anna Nye, Miss........... ....523 N. Delaware st.
Stanley Levi D., Mr. and Mrs.............318 N. Delaware st.
Stanley Lillian, Miss ....318 N. Delaware st.
Stanley John M., Mr......................318 N. Delaware st.
Stansbury Marcus L., Mr. and Mrs............70 W. 10th st.
Stansbury Duncan M............... ....70 W. 10th st.
Stanbury James V., Mr. and Mrs...............109 Talbot st.
Stanley O. W., Mr. and Mrs.................24 W. North st.
Stechan Otto, Mr. and Mrs......................25 Christian st.
Stechan Frank, Mr. and Mrs......................231 College st.
Steele Wm. Thos., Mr. and Mrs.........727 N. Delaware st.

THE ELITE LIST.

Steele Theodore C., Mr. and Mrs..................................
................................Cor. Pennsylvania and 7th sts.
Steele Rembrant T............Cor. Pennsylvania and 7th sts.
Steele Thomas J., Mrs.............................. 273 E. Walnut st.
Steele Catherine, Miss. ....273 E. Walnut st.
Steele Susan, Miss..273 E. Walnut st.
Stein Theodore, Mr. and Mrs................... 230 Central ave.
Stephens Margaretta, Miss............240 N. Pennsylvania st.
Stern John M.. 462 N. Pennsylvania st.
Stetchen Otto, Mr. and Mrs............................25 Christian st.
Stevens T. M., Mr. and Mrs..............,,,,,,,,353 S. New Jersey st.
Stevens Geo. G., Mr. and Mrs.....................3 Woodruff pl.
Stevenson Henry F., Mr. and Mrs..............34 Central ave.
Stevenson John, Mr. and Mrs..............940 N. Meridian st.
Stevenson Wm. Eaton, Mr. and Mrs....708 N. Alabama st.
Stevenson Rebecca J., Mrs...............704 N. Pennsylvania st.
Stevenson Margaret, Miss..............704 N. Pennsylvania st.
Stevenson Benj., Mr............ ....704 N. Pennsylvania st.
Stewart Martha, Mrs....................... 530 N. Delaware st.
Stewart John H., Mrs.........................735 N. Meridian st.
Stewart Kate G., Miss........................735 N. Meridian st.
Stewart Chas. H., Mr....................................357 N. Illinois st.
Stewart Kerfoot W., Mr........................357 N. Illinois st.
Stewart Chas. G., Mr. and Mrs................357 N. Illinois st.
Stewart Susan D...357 N. Illinois st.
Stewart Nettie, Miss..............................30 W. Walnut st.
Stiltz Wm. Fred., Mr. and Mrs.................122 E. Pratt st.
Stockton Sarah, Dr............................ 227 N. Delaware st.
Stone Lynn, Mr. and Mrs....................320 N. Illinois st.
Stone Katherine, Miss...................790 N. Pennsylvania st.
Stone Richard F., Dr. and Mrs..........294 N. Tennessee st.

Stout George W., Mr. and Mrs............262 N. Meridian st.
Stout Benj. F., Mr............................262 N. Meridian st.
Stout Furman, Mr. and Mrs...........209 N. Pennsylvania st.
Stowell Myron A., Mrs...........................83 W. 5th st.
Stowell Mary. Miss...............................83 W. 5th st.
Stubbs Joseph H., Mr. and Mrs..................474 Park ave.
Stucky Thos. A., Dr. and Mrs............580 N. Alabama st.
Sullivan Geo. R., Mr. and Mrs...........414 N. Meridian st.
Sullivan Thos. L., Mr. and Mrs..........253 N. Tennessee st.
Swan Geo. E., Rev. and Mrs...St. Mary's Hall, Central st.
Swain Rachel, Dr..........................334 N. New Jersey st.
Swain David, Mr. and Mrs............880 N. Pennsylvania st.
Swain Edna, Miss.......................880 N. Pennsylvania st.
Swain Wm. T., Mr. and Mrs.................447 College st.
Swain Esther, Miss...............................447 College st.
Sweeney Andrew M., Mr. and Mrs........931 N. Illinois st.
Swiggett Carl, Mr. and Mrs.....................66 Talbot ave.
Swiggett Chas. H., Mr. and Mrs.........930 N. Meridian st.
Swiggett Walter, M. and Mrs.............279 N. Meridian st.
Syfers R. K., Mr. and Mrs................348 N. Tennessee st.

TAGGART Thos., Mr. and Mrs...410 N. Tennessee st.
Taggart Alexander, Mr. and Mrs........384 Park ave.
Talbott Wm. Houston, Mr............230 N. Pennsylvania st.
Talbott E. C., Mrs....................230 N. Pennsylvania st.
Talbott Ella Root, Mrs...............................The Milton.
Talbott Laura, Miss..................................The Milton.
Talbott Anna B., Miss................................The Milton.
Talbott Frank, Mr. and Mrs ....884 N. Pennsylvania st.
Talbott Mary A., Mrs......................159 Christian ave.
Talbot Richard L., Mr. and Mrs ....178 Christian ave.

Talbot Howard M., Mr..................178 Christian ave.
Talbot Richard L. Jr., Mr. and Mrs..........74 Christian ave.
Talbott George, Mr. and Mrs........870 N. Pennsylvania st.
Tanner Geo. G., Mr. and Mrs............250 N. Tennessee st.
Tanner Maria, Miss.....................250 N. Tennessee st.
Tarkington, Wm. S., Mr. and Mrs......477 N. Tennessee st.
Tarkington John S., Mr. and Mrs..598 N. Pennsylvania st.
Tarkington Booth, Mr................598 N. Pennsylvania st.
Taylor Wm. A., Mr. and Mrs ....336 Central ave.
Taylor Bessie E., Miss...........................336 Central ave.
Taylor Josephine, Miss.....................849 N. Illinois st.
Taylor Joseph E., Mr. and Mrs......463 N. Pennsylvania st.
Taylor George Bryan.................463 N. Pennsylvania st.
Taylor Franklin, Mr. and Mrs........1140 E. Washington st.
Taylor Mary, Miss......................1140 E. Washington st.
Taylor Clara A., Mrs....................434 N. Delaware st.
Taylor Mary, Miss........................434 N. Delaware st.
Taylor Maj. and Mrs.......................683 N. Delaware st.
Taylor Cora, Miss..........................683 N. Delaware st.
Taylor Wilbur, Mr.........................683 N. Delaware st.
Taylor Wm. W., Mr. and Mrs............679 N. Delaware st.
Taylor Mrs...............................474 N. Tennessee st.
Taylor Alice, Miss........................474 N. Tennessee st.
Taylor Harold, Mr. and Mrs..............581 N. Delaware st.
Taylor Wm. F., Rev. and Mrs...........475 N. Meridian st.
..............................Summer Residence, Pine Lake.
Tennis Wm. H., Mr. and Mrs............356 N. Meridian st.
Tennis Alva R., Mr.........................356 N. Meridian st.
Test Chas. Edward, Mr. and Mrs...........98 Woodruff pl.
Test Bertha, Miss........................81 W. Vermont st.
Thalman Isaac, Mr. and Mrs............733 N. Meridian st.

Thomas John, Mr..................................750 N. Meridian st.
Thomas Ada, Mrs...........................548 N. Tennessee st.
Thomas Evan C., Mr. and Mrs................38 Woodruff pl.
Thomas James E., Mr. and Mrs...............38 Woodruff pl.
Thomas Evan C., Mr............................38 Woodruff pl.
Thomas Harry Edwin.........................38 Woodruff pl.
Thomas Albert D., Mr. and Mrs..............19 Woodruff pl.
Thomas Wm. Henry, Mr. and Mrs............420 College st.
Thompson Arthur N., Rev. and Mrs...........88 Pleasant st.
Thompson John W., Mr. and Mrs............86 Fletcher ave.
Thompson Kate A., Miss......................86 Fletcher ave.
Thompson Gideon B., Mr. and Mrs...........460 College st.
Thompson Frank H., Mr. and Mrs...........460 College st.
Thompson Edward C., Mr. and Mrs..........University ave.
Thompson Sara, Mrs ....248 N. East st.
Thompson Daniel A., Dr......................139 N. Illinois st.
Thompson James T., Dr. and Mrs..........139 N. Illinois st.
Thompson James L., Dr......................134 N. Illinois st.
Thompson Chas., Mr. and Mrs......874 N. Pennsylvania st.
Thompson Edward P., Mr. and Mrs..........278 Central ave.
Thompson Caroline, Miss.......................278 Central ave.
Thompson Blanche, Miss........................278 Central ave.
Thompson Thomas, Mr. and Mrs......940 N. Tennessee st.
Thompson Wm. C., Mr. and Mrs................73 W. Ohio st.
Thompson Thomas T., Dr. and Mrs..Julian ave., Irvington.
Thompson Levina, Mrs............................53 Ruckle st.
Thornton Matilda I., Mrs.......................374 College ave.
Thornton Henry Clark, Mr. and Mrs...831 N. Delaware st.
Thornton Chas. E., Mr. and Mrs ....236 Broadway.
Thrasher Wm. M., Mr. and Mrs....Washington, Irvington.
Tibbott David, Mr. and Mrs...........Ritter ave., Irvington.

Tibbott Anna, Miss.....................Ritter ave., Irvington.
Tibbott Vida, Miss.......................Ritter ave., Irvington.
Tibbott E. C., Mr. and Mrs............................Irvington.
Todd Margaret M., Mrs...........................597 N. Illinois st.
Todd L. L., Dr. and Mrs....................294 N. Alabama st.
Todd Susan, Miss............................294 N. Alabama st.
Todd Lizzie N., Miss........................ 294 N. Alabama st.
Todd Margaret, Miss........................294 N. Alabama st.
Todd Newton, Mr............................ 157 Bellefontaine st.
Tompkins J. H., Mr. and Mrs ....Irvington.
Tompkins John, Mr...................................Irvington.
Tompkins Bessie, Miss................................Irvington.
Tousey Eudora, Mrs ....359 N. Illinois st.
Tousey Hannah A., Miss....................359 N. Illinois st.
Townley George, Mr. and Mrs...................358 Broadway.
Townley Morris, Mr.............................. 358 Broadway.
Townsend Robert, Mr. and Mrs.....................490 Ash st.
Townsend Samuel, Mr. and Mrs ....20 W. 1st st.
Trask George K., Mr. and Mrs ....815 N. Meridian st.
Treat Atwater, Jr., Mr. and Mrs.........297 N. Meridian st.
Treat Edward L., Mr............................297 N. Meridian st.
Travis David I., Rev............................79 Woodburn ave.
Tucker Hannibal S., Mr. and Mrs.......341 N. Delaware st.
Turpie David, Senator......................173 N. Tennessee st.
Tutewiler Henry W., Mr. and Mrs...401 N. Mississippi st.
Tutewiler Henry W. Jr., Mr............401 N. Mississippi st.
Tuttle Benjamin, Mr.................................The Dennison.
Tyler Rebecca, Mrs.........................340 N. Meridian st.

UPFOLD Emily, Miss................546 Meridian st.

VAJEN Willis C., Mr. and Mrs...............
..........22 E. Vermont st., Martha's Vineyard.
Vajen John H., Mr. and Mrs...............128 N. Meridian st.
Vajen Frank, Mr...................128 N. Meridian st.
.........Spring Beach Cottage, Lake Maxinkucku, Ind.
Valodin Chas. M., Mr..........................The Milton.
Valodin John F., Mr....................Highland ave., (N. I.)
Van Buren Wm. A., Mr. and Mrs........746 N. Alabama st.
Van Buren Harriet, Mrs....................746 N. Alabama st.
Van Buskirk Daniel R., Rev..................294 College ave.
Van Buskirk Grace, Miss.................. 294 College ave.
Van Buskirk Harry W.....cor. Washington and Tennessee.
Van Camp Cortland, Mr. and Mrs......714 N. Delaware st.
Van Camp Raymond P ....714 N. Delaware st.
Van Camp Gilbert C., Mr. and Mrs.....926 Pennsylvania st.
Vance Herman C., Mr....................78 W. 10th st.
Van Hoff Henry L., Mr. and Mrs.........621 N. Meridian st.
Van Hummel Quincy, Dr. and Mrs..297 N. Pennsylvania st.
Van Hummel Henry, Dr..............297 N. Pennsylvania st.
Van Valkenburg, Miss..................621 N. Meridian st.
Van Vorhis Flavius J., Mr. and Mrs..276 N. Mississippi st.
Varney A. L., Major and Mrs.....................U. S. Arsenal.
Vinton Merrick E., Mr. and Mrs... 770 N. Pennsylvan'a st.
Vinton Thomas M., Mr............... 770 N. Pennsylvania st.
Vinnedge John A., Mr. and Mrs.........576 N. Alabama st.
Vinnedge Katharine, Miss................576 N. Alabama st.
Von Hake Carl, Mr. and Mrs................358 Park ave.
Vonnegut Clemens, Mr. and Mrs......... ..504 E. Market st.

Vonnegut Clemens, Jr., Mr. and Mrs ....224 Broadway.
Vonnegut Franklin, Mr........................508 E. Market st.
Vories Hervey, Mr. and Mrs..........179 N. Pennsylvania st.
Voss Jay G., Mr. and Mrs.................455 N. Meridian st.
Voss Tarquinna L., Miss............................Bates House.

WAGNER Abraham, Mr. and Mrs...238 Central ave.
Waite Ella M., Miss......599 N. Pennsylvania st.
Waite, Mr. and Mrs......................532 N. Delaware st.
Wainright John, Mr. and Mrs........866 N. Pennsylvania st.
Walcott Chas. H., Mr. and Mrs ....567 N. Illinois st.
Walcott Benj. D., Mr. and Mrs......777 N. Pennsylvania st.
Wallace M. S., Mrs.....................147 N. Pennsylvania st.
Wallace Henry L., Mr. and Mrs....749 N. Pennsylvania st.
Wallace David, Mr. and Mrs ....81 W. Vermont st.
Wallick Samuel, Mr. and Mrs................476 N. Illinois st.
Wallick John F., Mr. and Mrs.........⎫
Wallick John Glenn, Mr................ ⎪ 496 N. Meridian st.
Wallick Mary Glenn....................... ⎬ Summer Res.,
Wallick Adele, Miss....................... ⎪ Lake Maxinkuckee.
Wallick Katharine P., Miss............ ⎪
Wallick Martin H., Mr .... ⎭
Wales Samuel W., Mr. and Mrs...............250 College ave.
Wales Ruama, Miss...................................250 College ave.
Walk Julius C., Mr. and Mrs....................175 N. West st.
Walker Chas. M., Mr. and Mrs.....................76 W. 3d st.
Walker Helen Clair, Miss..............................76 W. 3d st.
Walker Ivan N., Mr. and Mrs............597 N. Tennessee st.
Walker Layton C., Mr........................597 N. Tennessee st.
Walker Sara J., Miss..........................597 N. Tennessee st.
Walker Thomas, Mr. and Mrs...........340 N. Tennessee st.
Walker Isaac C., Dr. and Mrs........130 N. Pennsylvania st.

Walker Frank, Mr..........................130 N. Pennsylvania st.
Walker Barclay, Mr. and Mrs..................34 W. North st.
Walker Lewis C., Judge and Mrs.. 429 N. Pennsylvania st.
Wands Wm., Mr. and Mrs..................408 N. Delaware st.
Wappenhaus Chas. F. R., Mr....................Ingalls Block.
Ward Albert L., Rev and Mrs........................110 Elm st.
Warman Enoch, Mr. and Mrs..............168 E. St. Clair st.
Warman Nancy, Miss........................ 168 E. St. Clair st.
Warman Enoch, Mr. and Mrs.............588 N. Alabama st.
Warman Nancy, Miss.......................588 N. Alabama st.
Warman Franklin E............................588 N. Alabama st.
Warne Joseph B., Mr. and Mrs.............16 W. Michigan st.
Warner Chas. F., Mr. and Mrs..............934 N. Illinois st.
Warren Hiram, Mr. and Mrs..............675 N. Delaware st.
Warren Grace, Miss..........................675 N. Delaware st.
Warren Fred., Mr..............................675 N. Delaware st.
Wason Wm. G., Mr. and Mrs..............21 W. Drive (W. P.)
Wasson Bertha Elizabeth, Miss...........21 W. Drive (W. P.)
Wasson Emma, Miss...........................21 W. Drive (W. P.)
Waters Patrick J., Dr.............................. Insane Asylum.
Watren Chauncey R., Mr. and Mrs............28 Morrison st
Watkinson James Lilly, Mr. and Mrs......398 N. Illinois st.
Watson Phil. Mitchell, Mr.................. 754 N. Delaware st.
Weaver Orzo D., Mr. and M:s.................857 N. Illinois st.
Webb Arthur H., Mr. and Mrs.................. ...440 Park ave.
Webb W. S., Mrs................................440 N. Meridian st.
Webb Courtland D., Mr. and Mrs.........440 N. Meridian st.
Weber Joseph F., Rev. and Mrs...............76 W. Georgia st.
Webster Frederick, Mr. and Mrs.........1667 N. Meridian st.
Webster George C., Mr. and Mrs..............574 College ave.
Webster Anna Miss............................706 N. Illinois st.

Webster Miss..................................706 N. Illinois st.
Weed Henry, Mr. and Mrs..................480 N. Meridian st.
Welburn Alice, Miss...........................985 N. Meridian st.
Weisenberger Lewis, Mr. and Mrs.......731 N. Delaware st.
Wellner Chas. H., Mr. and Mrs.............77 Woodruff pl.
Wellner Chas. E., Mr. and Mrs..............27 N. East st.
Wells Graham A., Dr. and Mrs.........181 N. New Jersey st.
Wells Merritt, Mrs...............................114 Broadway.
Wells Alexander E., Mr....................653 N. Pennsylvania st.
Wells Eleanor S., Miss......................653 N. Pennsylvania st.
Wells Margaret Miss........................653 N. Pennsylvania st.
Wells Miss..448 College ave.
Wells Chas. W., Mr. and Mrs...........221 N. New Jersey st.
Wells Livingston D., Mr..................221 N. New Jersey st.
West George Herman, Mr. and Mrs.772 N. Pennsylvania st.
West Bessie Marie, Miss..................772 N. Pennsylvania st.
Wetzel Henry, Mr. and Mrs...............200 N. Meridian st.
Wheeler Albert, Dr. and Mrs..................299 Broadway.
White Arthur C...................................257 N. Illinois st.
White Alma, Miss................................520 College ave.
White Geo. W., Mr.............................946 N. Tennessee st.
White Edwin F., Mr. and Mrs............946 N. Tennessee st.
White Daisy, Miss..............................946 N. Tennessee st.
Whitcomb Jerome G., Mr. and Mrs.566 N. Pennsylvania st.
Whitcomb Nellie C., Miss.............566 N. Pennsylvania st.
Whitcomb George E., Mr...............566 N. Pennsylvania st.
Whitehead Anna J., Mrs......................357 N. East st.
Whitehead Herbert L............................357 N. East st.
Whitney Alfred, Rev. and Mrs...............53 Fletcher ave.
Whittier D. L., Mr. and Mrs...............294 N. Meridian st.
Whittier A. G., Miss............................294 N. Meridian st.

Whitut John, Mr. and Mrs................809 N. Meridian st.
Wicks Alice B., Miss ....178 Christian ave.
Wiegand Anthony, Mr. and Mrs............844 N. Illinois st.
Wiggins Joseph P., Mrs....................700 N. Meridian st.
Wiggins Dudley Howard, Mr..............700 N. Meridian st.
Wilbrandt Emil, Mr. and Mrs.............67 Woodruff place.
Wildlock Wm. A., Mr. and Mrs..............201 Broadway.
Wildman James A., Mr. and Mrs...415 N. Pennsylvania st.
Wildman Anna, Miss ....415 N. Pennsylvania st.
Wiles Ernest, Mr. and Mrs..............428 N. Tennessee st.
Wiles Josephine, Mrs....................424 N. Delaware st.
Wiles Winnie Herman. ....424 N. Delaware st.
Wiles Daniel Hough, Mr. and Mrs........28 N. Vermont st.
Wiles Fred. Butler, Mr...................28 N. Vermont st.
Wiles Addie M...........................28 N. Vermont st.
Wiles Lulie Delle........................28 N. Vermont st.
Wiles Wm. D., Mr. and Mrs.............. 630 W. Illinois st.
Wiley David G., Mr. and Mrs...................221 N. East st.
Wiley Eliza G., Mrs...............477 N. Pennsylvania st.
Wiley Thomas, Mr. and Mrs..............400 N. Illinois st.
Wilkes Amy A., Mrs......................282 Central ave.
Wilkins John A., Mr. and Mrs.................396 Broadway.
Wilkins Albert..........................396 Broadway.
Wilkinson Allen A., Mr. and Mrs..........861 N. Illinois st.
Wilkinson Bessie, Miss................129 E. St. Joseph st.
Willard Albert L., Mr....................20 W. First st.
Williams Daniel G., Mr. and Mrs.....1094 N. Tennessee st.
Williams Oscar A., Rev....................33 Elm st.
Williams David R., Mr....................210 N. Meridian st.
Williams Chas. C., Mr. and Mrs........567 W. Michigan st.
Williams Walter Owen, Mr................101 Talbott ave.

Williams Chas. R., Mr. and Mrs..........567 N. Delaware st.
Williamson John A., Mrs............ Flats on Pennsylvania st.
Williamson Mary A., Miss.........Flats on Pennsylvania st.
Wilson John R., Mr. and Mrs ....174 Central ave.
Wilson J. H., Mrs............................466 N. Meridian st.
Wilson Drusilla, Mrs..................................446 Park ave.
Wilson John W., Rev. and Mrs.........................1 Vine st.
Wilson Medford B., Mr. and Mrs ....684 Delaware st.
Wilson Daisy, Miss............................. 684 Delaware st.
Wilson Sarah, Miss............................. 684 Delaware st.
Wilson Ruth, Miss...........................684 Delaware st.
Wilson Omar, Mr. and Mrs............Ritter ave., Irvington.
Wilson Francenia, Mrs...............................Irvington.
Wilson Blanche, Miss...................................Irvington.
Wilson James Higgins, Mr. and Mrs... 818 N. Alabama st.
Winn Lucius, Mr. and Mrs............134 N. Pennsylvania st.
Winslow Wm. W., Mr. and Mrs..........950 N. Meridian st.
Winsor George A., Mr ....86 W. 2d st.
Winsor Emma, Mrs.................................86 W. 2d st.
Winsor Marie...86 W. 2d st.
Winters Fred., Mr. and Mrs...............699 N. Meridian st.
Winters Kate, Miss............................699 N. Meridian st.
Winters Sue, Miss.............................699 N. Meridian st.
Winters Thomas, Mr...................... 699 N. Meridian st.
Winters James, Mr. and Mrs ....270 N. Illinois st.
Winings Daniel, Mr. and Mrs........820 N. Pennsylvania st.
Wishard Wm. H., Dr. and Mrs....................89 Huron st.
Wishard Elizabeth, Miss............................89 Huron st.
Wishard Harriet, Miss...............................89 Huron st.
Wishard Albert W., Mr..............................89 Huron st.
Wishard Wm. N., Dr ....89 Huron st.

Wocher John, Mr. and Mrs..............505 N. Delaware st.
Wocher Julius, Mr. and Mrs................681 Alabama st.
Wood W. A., Judge and Mrs....................The Dennison.
Wood Alice, Miss................................. The Dennison.
Wood Frank Morley................................539 Broadway.
Wood Frank, Mr. and Mrs....................62 Talbott ave.
Woodman A. C., Mr. and Mrs............619 N. Meridian st.
Wood Chas. H., Mr. and Mrs..............224 N. Meridian st.
Woods George W., Mr. and Mrs.........262 N. Alabama st.
Wood Horace F., Mr. and Mrs......848 N. Pennsylvania st.
Wood Daniel L., Mr. and Mrs .....417 N. Pennsylvania st.
Wood Willis G., Mr......... ....417 N. Pennsylvania st.
Wood Herbert S., Mr....................417 N. Pennsylvania st.
Wood Edson L., Mr......................417 N. Pennsylvania st.
Wood Marcia M., Miss................417 N. Pennsylvania st.
Wood John M., Mr. and Mrs.............187 Pennsylvania st.
Woolen Green V., Dr. and Mrs ....50 N. 12th st.
Woollen Wm. Watson, Mr. and Mrs.828 N. Pennsylvania st.
Woollen Marie, Miss ....828 N. Pennsylvania st.
Woollen Evans, Mr......................828 N. Pennsylvania st.
Woollen Harry, Mr......................828 N. Pennsylvania st.
Woolpert Marie, Miss........................83 E. Michigan st.
Wright James T., Mr. and Mrs...........697 N. Delaware st.
Wright John Cook, Mr. and Mrs...........30 E. Vermont st.
Wulschner Emil, Mr. and Mrs.............. Glen Flora Farm,
    ....Mooresville, Ind.
Wulsen Clarence, Mr. and Mrs............712 N. Meridian st.
Wunegut Bernard, Mr. and Mrs............. 342 Home ave.
Wymond H. A., Mr. and Mrs....................The Dennison.
Wymond Chas. F., Mr. and Mrs..... ..384 N. Tennessee st.

YANDES Geo. B., Mr..................84 E. Michigan.
Yandes Geo. B..........................The Dennison.
Yandes Simon..........................Grand Hotel.
Yohn James C., Mrs...........214 N. Delaware st.
Yohn Miss..............................214 N. Delaware st.
Young Archibald A., Mr. and Mrs......948 N. Tennessee st.

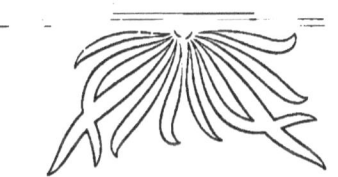

THE ELITE LIST.

PART II.
ARRANGED BY STREETS.

ALABAMA STREET.

100	Mr. Frederick Baggs	681	Mr. Julius Wocher
	Mrs. Frederick Baggs		Mrs. Julius Wocher
	Mr. Thomas B. Baggs	701	Mr. DeWitt C. Griffith
580	Mrs. Harriet Cox		Mrs. DeWitt C. Griffith

ALABAMA STREET, NORTH.

60	Mr. N. N. Howley	206	Mr. Wilmer F. Christian
102	Dr. John R. Brown		Mrs. Wilmer F. Christian
	Mrs. John R. Brown		Harry E. Christian
124	Dr. Wm. B. Fletcher		Wilmer F. Christian, Jr.
	Mrs. Wm. B. Fletcher	208	Mr. Nathan F. Dalton
	Miss Aileen D. Fletcher		Mrs. Nathan F. Dalton
	Miss Lucy Hines Fletcher		Mr. Charles Dalton
	Miss Una Cladys Fletcher	214	Mr. George J. Hammel
167	Mr. Samuel E. Bank		Mrs. George J. Hammel
	Mrs. Samuel E. Bank		Mr. Wm. W. Hammel
177	Mr. James E. Robertson		Mr. George C. Hammel
	Mrs. James E. Robertson		

ALABAMA STREET, NORTH.—Continued.

232 Mr. Charles Moores
Mrs. Julia Moores
Miss Janet Moores
Mr. Merril Moores
250 Mr. Herman Leiber
Mrs. Herman Leiber
Mr. Carl Leiber
256 Mr. Ad. Hereth
Mrs. Ad. Hereth
Miss Lulu M. Hereth
262 Mr. George W. Woods
Mrs. George W. Woods
266 Rev. Albert A. Ogle
Mrs. Albert A. Ogle
Mr. Robert C. Ogle
294 Dr. L. L. Todd
Mrs. L. L. Todd
Miss Susan Todd
Miss Lizzie N. Todd
Miss Margaret Todd
366 Mr. John W. Smith
Mrs. John W. Smith
478 Mr. Geo. P. Marott
Mrs. Geo. P. Marott
570 Mr. Wm. M. Johnston
Mrs. Wm. M. Johnston
Miss Blanche Johnston
576 Mr. John A. Vinnedge
Mrs. John A. Vinnedge
Miss Katherine Vinnedge
580 Dr. Thos. A. Stucky
Mrs. Thos. A. Stucky
588 Mr. Enoch Warman
Mrs. Enoch Warman
Miss Nancy Warman
Franklin E. Warman

596 Mr. Wm. Henry Potter
Mrs. Wm. Henry Potter
Lilian P. Potter
600 Miss Laura Ream
Mrs. Diantha Dunlap
Miss Elizabeth Dunlap
Livingston Dunlap
604 Mr. Sam. A. Haines
Mrs. Sam. A. Haines
Miss Ella E. Haines
622 Mr. Henry Clay Adams
Mrs. Henry Clay Adams
Henry Clay Adams, Jr.
648 Mr. Enthrakin T. Hibben
Mrs. Enthrakin T. Hibben.
650 Miss Ruby Almeda Rees
656 Mr. Albert Michie
Mrs. Albert Michie
672 Mr. John S. Duncan
Miss Agnes Duncan
Wallace Duncan
677 Mr. Frederick A. Davis
Mrs. Frederick A. Davis
G. Davis
Miss Lusette Davis
Mr. Hugh McK. Landon
Mrs. Hugh McK. Landon
682 Mr. Ellsworth Parrott
Mrs. Ellsworth Parrott
683 Rev. John W. Dashiel
Mrs. John W. Dashiel
698 Mr. Herman Dewenter
Mrs. Herman Dewenter
Miss Millie Dewenter
699 Miss May Johnson

THE ELITE LIST.

ALABAMA STREET, NORTH.—Continued.

700 Mr. Frederick M. Herron
Mrs. Frederick M. Herron
Miss Mary Herron
Miss Lydia Herron
Miss Josephine B. Herron
Fred. P. Herron
Walter Herron
Miss Katharine Herron
705 Mr. Wm. H. Cook
Mrs. Wm. H. Cook
707 Miss Mary A. Jones
708 Mr. Wm. Eaton Stevenson
Mrs. Wm. Eaton Stevenson
710 Mr. Liberty C. McLain
Mrs. Liberty C. McLain
715 Mr. Wm. Henry Hobbs
Mrs. Wm. Henry Hobbs
744 Mr. John McRenna
Mrs. John McRenna
Miss Laura McRenna
746 Mr. Wm. A. Van Buren
Mrs. Wm. A. Van Buren
Mrs. Harriet Van Buren
750 Mr. Wm. Park Kappes
Mrs. Wm. Park Kappes
765 Mr. Bertrand Adams
Mrs. Bertrand Adams

766 Mr. Sam. S. Rhodes
Mrs. Sam. S. Rhodes
Mr. Clarence R. Rhodes
768 Mr. Harry A. Crossland
Mrs. Harry A. Crossland
769 Dr. Holton
Mrs. Holton
772 Mr. Silas Schepard
Mrs. Silas Schepard
Mr. Frank Schepard
Silas Schepard, Jr.
Harriet A. Schepard
787 Mr. Frank D. Macbeth
Mrs. Frank D. Macbeth
Miss Edna Macbeth
Miss Dare Macbeth
814 Mr. John Chestnutt
Mrs. John Chestnutt
818 Mr. James Higgins Wilson
Mrs. James Higgins Wilson
870 Mr. John A. Goulding
Mrs. John A. Goulding
872 Mr. John Wm. Coons
Mrs. John Wm. Coons
874 Mr. Henry Clay Allen
Mrs. Henry Clay Allen
958 Miss Agnes E. Rankin
Miss Louise Rankin

ASH STREET.

411 Mr. Wm. D. Bynum
Mrs. Wm. D. Bynum
413 Miss Elizabeth K. Jameson
Miss Betty Jameson

459 Mr. Clarence Forsyth
Mrs. Clarence Forsyth
527 Mr. James T. Eaglesfield
Mrs. James T. Eaglesfield

THE ELITE LIST. 95

BROADWAY.

114	Mrs. Merritt Wells	316	Mr. Claud T. Griffith
164	Mrs. Mary Bond		Mrs. Claud T. Griffith
	Miss Mary E. Bond	324	Mr. Edward Hawkins
188	Miss Charity Dye		Mrs. Edward Hawkins
	Miss May Dye		Mr. Don Hawkins
193	Elizabeth G. Hughes	328	Dr. Wm. Allison
199	Mr. John Spann		Mrs. Wm. Allison
	Mrs. John Spann	329	Mrs. Jennie H. Maguire
200	Judge Edgar A. Brown		Mr. Albert M. Maguire
	Mrs. Edgar A. Brown	341	Mrs. Louise O. Robinson
201	Mr. Wm. H. Wildlock		Dr. Wilbur S. Robinson
	Mrs. Wm. H. Wildlock		Miss L. Jenkins Robinson
209	Mr. Harry H. Friendly	342	Mr. Lew Wallace Cooper
	Mrs. Harry H. Friendly		Mrs. Lew Wallace Cooper
210	Mr. John M. Commons	350	Mr. Oscar D. Bohlen
	Mrs. John M. Commons		Mrs. Oscar D. Bohlen
224	Mr. Clemens Vonnegut, Jr.	357	Mr. Frank McCrea
	Mrs. Clemens Vonnegut, Jr.		Mrs. Frank McCrea
236	Mr. Chas. E. Thornton		Rolin Hall McCrea
	Mrs. Chas. E. Thornton	358	Mr. George Townley
242	Mr. Julius J. Higgins		Mrs. George Townley
	Mrs. Julius J. Higgins		Mr. Morris Townley
249	Mr. Horace McKay	361	Mr. Railey Jordan
	Mrs. Horace McKay		Mrs. Railey Jordan
	Miss Mary McKay		Mrs. Sarah J. Hagarth
	Miss Cornelia McKay	373	Dr. Lehman Dunning
292	Mr. Fred. Gardner		Mrs. Lehman Dunning
	Mrs. Fred. Gardner	378	Mr. Chas. J. Kuhn
299	Dr. Albert Wheeler	381	Mr. James Q. Barcus
	Mrs. Albert Wheeler		Mrs. James Q. Barcus
300	Mr. Frederick Kuhn	387	Mr John J. Appel
	Mrs. Frederick Kuhn		Mrs. John J. Appel
315	Mr. Joseph Jewar	388	Mr. Barton W. Cole
	Mrs. Joseph Jewar		Mrs. Barton W. Cole

BROADWAY.—Continued.

395 George W. Powell
Fred. D. Powell
396 Mr. Frank W. Armstrong
Mrs Frank W. Armstrong
Mr. John A. Wilkins
Mrs. John A. Wilkins
Albert Wilkins
412 Mrs. Frances Bohlen
. Mrs. Augusta Martin
433 Mr. Chas. Humphrey
Mrs. Chas. Humphrey
433 M. Hervey Humphrey
440 Mr. Wm. C. Bobbs
Mrs. Wm. C. Bobbs
443 James B. Sidener
449 Mr. Granville G. Allen
Mrs. Granville G. Allen
465 Mr. Augustus Herzsch
Mrs. Augustus Herzsch
492 Mr. Howard Cale
Mrs. Howard Cale
525 Miss Francis Branton

CENTRAL AVENUE.

18 Mr. John W. Dittemore
Miss Mabelle Dittemore
28 Mr. Wm. A. Applegate
Mrs. Wm. A. Applegate
Wm. H. Applegate
32 Mr. M. O'Connor
Mrs. M. O'Connor
Mr. Joseph S. O'Connor
Edward J. O'Connor
52 Mr. Thos. O'Neil Morris
Mrs. Thos. O'Neil Morris
Mr. Chester Morris
100 Mr. Thos. A. Morris
Mr. John I. Morris
103 Mr. John A. Kurtz
Mrs. John A. Kurtz
165 Mr. Henry Schnull
Mrs. Henry Schnull
209 Mr. Robert N. Lamb
Mrs. Robert N. Lamb
Miss Marietta Lamb
233 Mr. Daniel L. Dorsey
Mr. Robert L. Dorsey
Mrs. Robert L. Dorsey
Mrs. Katharine L. Dorsey
Frank O. Dorsey
236 Mr. George F. Gooking
Mrs. George F. Gooking
246 Mr. Samuel Phillips
Mrs. Samuel Phillips
268 Mr. Robert M. Furnas
Mrs. Robert M. Furnas
270 Rev. C. S. Sargent
Mrs. C. S. Sargent
Mr. James F. T. Sargent
274 Mr. Wm. S. Budd
Mrs. Wm. S. Budd
Miss Rose Martha Budd
278 Mr. Edward P. Thompson
Mrs. Edward P. Thompson
Miss Caroline Thompson
Miss Blanche Thompson

THE ELITE LIST.

CENTRAL AVENUE.—Continued.

288	Mr. Wm. McK. Graydon	368	Mr. Chas. A. Dryer
	Mrs. Wm. McK. Graydon		Mrs. Chas. A. Dryer
	Miss Mary M. Graydon	432	Mr. Oliver S. Dale
	Miss Katharine Graydon		Mrs. Oliver S. Dale
	Miss Jean Graydon		Mr. Burnam C. Dale
	Mr. Douglas Graydon	435	Mr. August Dietrich
331	Dr. Wm. S. Haskell		Mrs. August Dietrich
	Mrs. Wm. S. Haskell	444	Dr. Clinton E. Galloway
336	Mr. Wm. A. Taylor		Mrs. Clinton E. Galloway
	Mrs. Wm. A. Taylor	445	Mr. Amos Reagon
	Miss Bessie E. Taylor		Mrs. Amos Reagon

CHRISTIAN AVENUE.

24	Mr. Albert Rabb	177	Mr. C. A. Heath
	Mrs. Albert Rabb		Mrs. C. A. Heath
25	Mr. Otto Stechan	178	Mr. Arthur Boothby
	Mrs. Otto Stechan		Mrs. Arthur Boothby
30	Mr. Albert J. Beveridge		Mr. Richard L. Talbot
	Mrs. Albert J. Beveridge		Mrs. Richard L. Talbot
33	Mr. John W. Baird		Miss Alice B. Wicks
	Mrs. John W. Baird		Mr. Howard M. Talbot
74	Mr. Richard L. Talbot, Jr	204	Mr. Wm. L. O'Connor
	Mrs. Richard L. Talbot, Jr		Mrs. Wm. L. O'Connor
159	Mr. James J. Fletcher	221	Mr. Allen Bell
	Mrs. James J. Fletcher		Mrs. Allen Bell
	Mrs. Mary A. Talbott		Miss Jessie Bell
170	Mrs. Margaret Marshall		

COLLEGE AVENUE.

224	Mr. Wm. B. Barry	235	Mr. James M. Cropsey
	Mrs. Wm. B. Barry		Mrs. James M. Cropsey
231	Mr. Frank Stechan		Miss Nebraska Cropsey
	Mrs. Frank Stechan	250	Mr. Samuel W. Wales

COLLEGE AVENUE.—Continued.

250 Mrs. Samuel W. Wales
Miss Ruama Wales
294 Rev. Dan'l R. Van Buskirk
Miss Grace Van Buskirk
308 Mr. Wm. Henley
Mrs. Wm. Henley
Miss Effie Henley
311 Mr. John B. Cochrum
Mrs. John B. Cochrum
317 Mr. Wm. H. Schoppenhorst
Mrs. Wm. H. Schoppenhorst
340 Mr. Chas. W. Smith
Mrs. Chas. W. Smith
Miss Jennie Smith
349 Mr. John Lyon
Mrs. John Lyon
Miss Daisy Lyon
Miss Elizabeth Lyon
Mr. Frederick Lyon
Mr. Luther W. Lyon
350 Mr. Wm. Dawson Cooper
Mrs. Wm. Dawson Cooper
Miss Eliz. Ingram Cooper

354 Mr. Lewis V. Boyle
Mrs. Lewis V. Boyle
374 Mr. Robert M. King
Mrs. Robert M. King
Mr. Chas. W. Lefler
Mrs. Chas. W. Lefler
Curtis Harris Lefler
Mrs. Matilda I. Thornton
447 Mr. Wm. T. Swain
Mrs. Wm. T. Swain
Miss Esther Swain
448 Mr. Henry Butler
Mrs. Henry Butler
Miss Wells
492 Miss Anna Pyle
520 Miss Alma White
574 Mr. Geo. C. Buck
Mrs. Geo. C. Buck
Miss Maud Buck
639 Mr. James B. Heywood
Mrs. James B. Heywood
825 Mr. Henry A. Buchtel
Mrs. Henry A. Buchtel
Mr. Frost Croft Buchtel

DELAWARE STREET, NORTH.

165 Mr. Frank W. Lee
Mrs. Frank W. Lee
172 Mr. Samuel Compton
Mrs. Samuel Compton
195 Dr. Joseph Eastman
Mrs. Joseph Eastman
Mr. Joseph Rilus Eastman
Dr. Thomas Eastman
Mrs. Thomas Eastman
Miss Mary Eastman

214 Mrs. James C. Yohn
Miss Yohn
216 Miss Eleanor Ketcham
Miss Elizabeth Ketcham
227 Dr. Sarah Stockton
243 Mr. Myron D. King
Mrs. Myron D. King
257 Dr. Edwin Rufus
Mrs. Edwin Rufus
Mr. Lewis Rufus

THE ELITE LIST.

DELAWARE STREET, NORTH.—Continued.

270 Dr. Evan Hadley
Mrs. Evan Hadley
Mr. Chalmers Hadley
275 Mr. Geo. B. Hall
Mrs. Geo. B. Hall
Mrs. Ella Bush McCay
276 Mr. John R. Knight
Mrs. John R. Knight
Miss Louise Knight
277 Mrs. Oscar Wilson Sears
Mrs. Isabel M. Adams
288 Mr. T. Volney Malott
Mrs. T. Volney Malott
Miss Florence M. Malott
Miss Carrie G. Malott
Miss Laura Malott
Miss Katharine Malott
297 Mr. Edwin A. Hendrickson
Mrs. Edwin A. Hendrickson
298 Mrs. David Macy
302 Mr. Alden Linton Cox
Mrs. Alden Linton Cox
Delitha B. Harvey
Kate P. Harvey
Mrs. Jessie Butler Harvey
306 Mr. Mahlon Butler
Mrs. Mahlon Butler
Samuel Lee Butler
307 Miss Fidelia Anderson
Mr. Albert B. McGregory
Mrs. Albert B. McGregory
317 Mr. Edward B. Morris
Mrs. Edward B. Morris
318 Mr. Levi D. Stanley
Miss Lillian Stanley

318 Mr. John M. Stanley
Mrs. Levi D. Stanley
323 Mr. Chas. F. Meyer
Mrs. Chas. F. Meyer
341 Mr. Hannibal S. Tucker
Mrs. Hannibal S. Tucker
373 Mr. Oscar W. Schmidt
Mrs. Elizabeth M. Schmidt
Mr. Edward H. Schmidt
Mr. Wm. H. Schmidt
390 Mrs. Stella Anderson
394 Mr. Wm. Hackerdon
Mrs. Wm. Hackerdon
420 Mr. Edward Reeves
Miss Reeves
Miss Lillian Reeves
421 Mr. Sam. W. McMahan
Mrs. Sam. W. McMahan
424 Mrs. Josephine Wiles
Winnie Herman Wiles
429 Mr. Chas. H. Comstock
Mrs. Chas. H. Comstock
434 Mrs. Clara A. Taylor
Miss Mary Taylor
437 Mr. Frank S. McBride
Mrs. Frank S. McBride
Mr. Stanley McBride
470 Mr. Wm. R. Evans
Mrs. Wm. R. Evans
Mr. Edward Evans
505 Mr. John Wocher
Mrs. John Wocher
506 Mr. Frank Hancock
Mrs. Ellen Hancock

DELAWARE STREET, NORTH.—Continued.

510 Mr. Frank A. Coffin
Mrs. Frank A. Coffin
517 Miss Maria Johnston
Mr. Richard Demsey Reeves
Mrs. Richard Demsey Reeves
518 Mr. Daniel U. Marmon
Mrs. Daniel U. Marmon
Mr. Walter C. Marmon
Mr. Howard C. Marmon
523 Howard M. Stanton
Mr. Ambrose P. Stanton
Mrs. Ambrose P. Stanton
Miss Anna Nye Stanton
525 Dr. Fred. O. Clemmer
Mrs. Fred. O. Clemmer
532 Mr. Waite
Mrs. Waite
534 Mr. Wm. H. Griffith
Mrs. Wm. H. Griffith
536 Mr. Alpheus Snow
Mrs. Alpheus Snow
540 Mr. Joseph P. Shipp
566 Mrs. Annie E. Root
567 Mr. Chas. R. Williams
Mrs. Chas. R. Williams
580 Mr. Enrique C. Miller
Mrs. Enrique C. Miller
581 Mr. Aaron H. Blair
Mrs. Aaron H. Blair
584 Mr. Fred. Mayer
Mrs. Fred. Mayer
585 Mr. James F. Failey
Mrs. James F. Failey
Miss Alice Failey
Mr. Bruce Failey

599 Mr. John T. Dye
Mrs. John T. Dye
Miss Annie Dye
Miss Elizabeth F. Dye
Maizie Bacon Dye
600 Mr. Julius Hanson
Mrs. Julius Hanson
Miss Mary Hanson
601 Mr. George F. Seymour
Mrs. George F. Seymour
603 Miss Jennie Rafert
605 Mr. Addison Nardyke
Mrs. Addison Nardyke
Mr. Chas. E. Nardyke
Mr. Walter A. Nardyke
606 Mr. John M. Butler
Mrs. John M. Butler
John Maurice Butler
655 Mr. Chas. S. Millard
Mrs. Chas. S. Millard
656 Mr. Lyman S. Ayers
Mrs. Lyman S. Ayers
Mr. Fred. M. Ayers
665 Mr. Samuel Miller
Mrs. Samuel Miller
Mr. Wm. H. Miller
Mrs. Wm. H. Miller
Miss Jessie Miller
667 Mrs. Kate Perry Morris
Mr. John Calvin Perry
Mr. Thomas Arba Perry
673 Mr. Edward L. McKee
674 Mr. Benjamin F. Harrison
675 Mr. Hiram Warren
Mrs. Hiram Warren

DELAWARE STREET, NORTH.—Continued.

675	Miss Grace Warren	743	Mr. Harold Hibben
	Mr. Fred. Warren		Mrs. Harold Hibben
679	Dr. Horace R. Allen	750	Mr. Justus Cooley Adams
	Mrs. Horace R. Allen		Mrs. Justus Cooley Adams
	Horace R. Allen, Jr.		Fred. Bliss Adams
	Mr. Wm. W. Taylor	754	Mr. Phil. Mitchel Watson
	Mrs. Wm. W. Taylor	783	Mr. Leigh R. Baugher
683	Maj. Taylor		Mrs. Leigh R. Baugher
	Mrs. Taylor	785	Mr. Geo. W. Snider
	Miss Cora Taylor		Mrs. Geo. W. Snider
	Mr. Wilbur Taylor	831	Mr. Henry Clark Thornton
697	Mr. James T. Wright		Mrs. Henry Clark Thornton
	Mrs. James T. Wright	862	Mr. Chas. K. Mavity
714	Mr. Cortland Van Camp		Mrs. Chas. K. Mavity
	Mrs. Cortland Van Camp	863	Mr. George Pearson Cooper
	Raymond P. Van Camp		Mrs. George Pearson Cooper
725	Mr. Oran Perry	872	Judge James W. Harper
	Mrs. Oran Perry		Mrs. James W. Harper
727	Mr. Wm. Thos. Steele	873	Mr. Luther Benson
	Mrs. Wm. Thos. Steele		Mrs. Luther Benson
729	Mr. Wm. Knight	874	Mr. Willard Henry Coburn
729½	Mr. Alvia S. Lockhard		Mrs. Willard Henry Coburn
	Mrs. Cordelia B. Lockhard	876	Mr. Adelbert Benson
731	Mr. Lewis Weisenberger		Mrs. Adelbert Benson
	Mrs. Lewis Weisenberger	881	Dr. Wm. H. Kindleberger
733	Mr. Wm. P. Fishback		Mrs. Wm. H. Kindleberger
	Mrs. Wm. P. Fishback	911	Mr. Wm. M. Levey
735	Mr. Harvey J. Milligan		Mrs. Wm. M. Levey
	Mrs. Harvey J. Milligan	915	Mr. David T. Praig
740	Mr. John W. Schmidt		
	Mrs. John W. Schmidt		

EAST DRIVE, (W. P.)

147 Mr. Horace G. Coldwell
    Mrs. Horace G. Coldwell
180 Mr. Chester Barney
    Mrs. Chester Barney

180 Mrs. Laura Barney Nash
181 Mr. Russell McClellan Seeds
    Mrs. Russell McClellan Seeds

EAST STREET, NORTH.

27 Mr. Charles E. Wellner
    Mrs. Charles E. Wellner
205 Mr. Frank H. Blackledge
    Mrs. Frank H. Blackledge
232 Mr. Robert Graff
    Mrs. Robert Graff
243 Mr. Carl Barnes
    Mrs. Carl Barnes
248 Mr. Phillip J. Shaw
    Mrs. Phillip J. Shaw
    Mrs. Sara Thompson

310 Dr. Grove Anthony
    Dr. Emanuel Anthony
    Mrs. Emanuel Anthony
357 Mrs. Anna J. Whitehead
    Herbert L. Whitehead
    Mr. Reginald H. Giles
    Mr. Pleasant H. Griffith
372 Mr. John L. Moore
    Mrs. John L. Moore
    Miss Lillian Moore
401 Miss Sadie E. Reed

FLETCHER AVENUE.

53 Rev. Alfred Whitney
    Mrs. Alfred Whitney
86 Mr. John W. Thompson
    Mrs. John W. Thompson
    Miss Kate A. Thompson
114 Miss Selma M. Ingersoll
    Miss Henrietta Ingersoll
    Miss Mary Ingersoll

132 Mr. Elijah J. Forsyth
    Mr. Wm. J. Forsyth
    Miss Alice Forsyth
    Miss Elizabeth Forsyth
174 Mr. James Chambers
    Mrs. James Chambers

HOME AVENUE.

22 Mr. Cornelius B. Holloway
    Mrs. Cornelius B. Holloway
    Miss Ida M. Manly
23 Mrs. Theresa H. Smith
    Mr. Goldwin J. Smith
    Miss Gail Smith
24 Mrs. Anna L. Claypool
    Miss Jessie Clippenger
27 Mr. David E. Snyder
    Mrs. David E. Snyder
    Miss Alice May Snyder

131 Mr. August Meyer
    Mrs. August Meyer
308 Mr. Daniel M. Bradbury
    Mrs. Daniel M. Bradbury
342 Mr. Bernard Wunegut
    Mrs. Bernard Wunegut
375 Mr. Horace H. Fletcher
    Mrs. Horace H. Fletcher
376 Miss Emily Fletcher
379 Mr Calvin Fletcher
    Mrs. Calvin Fletcher
    Miss Emily Fletcher

ILLINOIS STREET, NORTH.

45 Mr. James E. Shaver
    Mrs. James E. Shaver
    Miss Shaver
134 Dr. John H. Oliver
    Mrs. John H. Oliver
139 Dr. James L. Thompson
    Dr. Daniel A. Thompson
    Dr. James T. Thompson
    Mrs. James T. Thompson
151 Dr. Elmer E. Cary
    Mrs. Elmer E. Cary
188 Mrs. Rebecca J. King
    Miss Emma B. King
    Mr. Roderick King
189 Mrs. Henry H. Lee
213 Dr. Dawson Barnes
    Mrs. Dawson Barnes
    Dr. Carl Barnes

222 Mr. Chas. Kenney
    Mrs. Chas. Kenney
    Mr. Nathaniel F. Morrow
    Mrs. Nathaniel F. Morrow
236 Mr. Lewis G. Hough
257 Arthur C. White
260 Mrs. Leah P. Ramsey
264 Dr. Jno. R. Haynes
    Mrs. Jno. R. Haynes
270 Judge Frederick Rand
279 Mr. Wilbur Hitt
    Mrs. Wilbur Hitt
285 Mr. Gustav Schmell
    Mrs. Gustav Schmell
292 Mr. Samuel E. Morse
    Mrs. Samuel E. Morse
    Mr. Lewis Herbert Morrell
    Mrs. Lewis Herbert Morrell

ILLINOIS STREET, NORTH.—Continued.

300 Mr. Raphael Kirschbaum
Mrs. R phael Kirschbaum
Miss May Kirschbaum
320 Mr. Lynn Stone
Mrs. Lynn Stone
347 Mr. Vincent G. Clifford
353 Rev. John H. Ketcham
Mrs. John H. Ketcham
357 Mr. Chas. H. Stewart
Mr. Kerfoot W. Stewart
Mr. Chas. G. Stewart
Mrs. Chas. G. Stewart
Susan D. Stewart
359 Mrs. Eudora Tousey
Miss Hanna A. Tousey
374 Mr. Albert Gall, Jr
Mrs. Albert Gall, Jr
376 Mr. Thomas D. Scott
Mrs. Thomas D. Scott
Miss Jane Scott
Miss Ray Scott
388 Dr. John T. Johnston
Mrs. John T. Johnston
398 Mr. Harry C. Dollens
Mr. Robert W. Dollens
Mrs. Robert W. Dollens
Mr. James Lilly Watkinson
Mrs. James Lilly Watkinson
400 Mr. Thomas Wiley
Mrs. Thomas Wiley
Mr. Wm. Judson
Mrs. Wm. Judson
Rev. Geo. G. Mitchell
Mrs. Geo. G. Mitchell
Miss Florence C. Mitchell

426 Mr. Frank R. New
Mrs. Frank R. New
Mr. Wm. Ellen Hicks
Mrs. Wm. Ellen Hicks
433 Mr. Nathan Scharff
Mrs. Nathan Scharff
476 Mr. Samuel Wallick
Mrs. Samuel Wallick
Mr. John Wade Dodd
Mrs. John Wade Dodd
482 John A. Craig
Mr. Charles A. Craig
489 Mr. C. B. Huston
Mrs. C. B. Huston
512 Mrs. Sarah J. Pattison
Mr. Day C. Pattison
Mr. Samuel L. Pattison
520 Dr. J. A. Consingor
Mrs. J. A. Consingor
526 Mr. Chas. Kahlo
Mrs. Chas. Kahlo
Dr. George Kahlo
Dr. Henry C. Kahlo
551 Mr. Edward Hill
Mrs. Edward Hill
554 Mr. Wm. H. Laird
Mrs. Wm. H. Laird
Wm. H. Laird, Jr
Mr. James H. Laird
556 Mr. John A. Allison
Mrs. John A. Allison
Mrs. Mary Augusta Binford
Mr. Carroll L. DeWitt
567 Mr. Chas. H. Walcott
Mrs. Chas. H. Walcott

ILLINOIS STREET, NORTH.—Continued.

577 Mr. Wm. H. Hubbard	705 Mr. John Madden
Mrs. Wm. H. Hubbard	Mr. E. J. O'Reilly
590 Mr. Albert Gall	Mrs. E. J. O'Reilly
Mrs Albert Gall	706 Miss Anna Webster
Miss Bertha Gall	724 Mr. Chas. C. Perry
597 Miss Mary Ann McLain	Mrs. Chas. C. Perry
600 Mr. Chas. Sumner Lewis	748 Mr. James W. Bryan
Mrs. Chas. Sumner Lewis	Mrs. James W. Bryan
613 Mr. Wm. E. Kurtz	Mr. Hugh Bryan
Mr. Irving S. Gordon	776 Mrs. Amanda J. Davis
639 Mr. Wm. L. Dunlap	782 Mr. Albert Barnes
Mrs. Wm. L. Dunlap	Mrs. Albert Barnes
640 Miss Florence E. Cutter	844 Mr. Anthony Wiegand
Frederick Page Cutter	Mrs. Anthony Wiegand
642 Mr. Alexander Heron	849 Miss Josephine Taylor
Mrs. Alexander Heron	Mrs. Agnes Basler
Miss Mary R. Heron	859 Miss Anna Fletcher
644 Mr. Henry Frank	Mr. Johnson Mendenhall
Mrs. Henry Frank	Mrs. Johnson Mendenhall
670 Mrs. Joseph K. Sharpe	861 Mr. S. R. Greer
Miss Julia G. Sharpe	Mr. Allen A. Wilkinson
Miss Anna T. Sharpe	Mrs. Allen A. Wilkinson
677 Mr. John E. Scott	863 Mr. Richard R. Reeves
Mrs. John E. Scott	Mrs. Richard R. Reeves
683 Mr. Frank Bird	Mr. Richard E. Reeves
Mrs. Frank Bird	888 Mr. Wm. Higbee Elvin
Miss Jessie Bird	Mrs. Wm. Higbee Elvin
685 Mr. Malcolm McDonald	Mr. Robert John Elvin
Mrs. Malcolm McDonald	Mrs. Robert John Elvin
Mr. Malcolm S. McDonald	890 Mr. Chas. E. Kregelo
688 Mr. Louis E. Francis	Mrs. Chas. E. Kregelo
Mrs. Louis E. Francis	Miss Katharine Kregelo
Miss Harriet Francis	894 Mr. John Andrew Cutting
705 Mr. Thomas Madden	Mrs. John Andrew Cutting
Mrs. Thomas Madden	

ILLINOIS STREET, NORTH.—Continued.

894	Mr. Joseph Crandall	996	Miss Mary Lilly
	Mrs. Joseph Crandall	1011	Mr. Harry Landis
909	Mr. Chas. W. Byfield		Miss Virginia M. Landis
	Arthur H. Byfield		Miss Katharine D. Landis
	Harry N. Byfield		Mr. John Landis
	Bessie C. Byfield	1015	Mr. Thos. H. Parry
	Emma C. Byfield		Mrs. Thos. H. Parry
922	Mr. Alex. McCleary	1038	Miss Louise Raschig
	Mrs. Alex. McCleary		Miss Florence Raschig
	Mr. Chas. A. McCleary		Mr. Chas. Raschig
	Mr. Hill T. McCleary	1042	Mr. Wm. Linden
923	Mr. J. C. Shoemaker		Mrs. Wm. Linden
	Mrs. J. C. Shoemaker	1044	Rev. Joseph S. Jenckes
	John C. Shoemaker		Mrs. Joseph S. Jenckes
931	Mr. Andrew M. Sweeney		Miss Jenckes
	Mrs. Andrew M. Sweeney	1053	Mr. Aquila Q. Jones
	Miss Carrie L. Kuebler		Mrs. Aquila Q. Jones
934	Mr. Chas. F. Warner	1055	Mr. Frank D. Stalnaker
	Mrs. Chas. F. Warner		Mrs. Frank D. Stalnaker
936	Mr. Henry D. Martin	1057	Mr. Nicholas R. Ruckle
	Miss Helen Martin		Mrs. Nicholas R. Ruckle
956	Oliver T. Byram	1063	Mr. Samuel D. Pray
	Henry G. Byram		Mrs. Samuel D. Pray
	Norman S. Byram	1088	Mr. Chester Bradford
988	Miss Emma J. Holloway		Mrs. Chester Bradford
	Mrs. Aquilla Jones		Mr. Ridgely B. Hilliary
996	Mr. James E. Lilly		Mrs. Ridgely B. Hilliary
	Mrs. James E. Lilly		

THE ELITE LIST.

MERIDIAN STREET, NORTH.

103 Dr. Herman Pink
    Mrs. Herman Pink
128 Mr. Samuel H. Collins
    Mrs. Samuel H. Collins
    Mr. John H. Vajen
    Mrs. John H. Vajen
    Mr. Frank Vajen
134 Dr. Louis M. Rowl
    Mrs. Louis M. Rowl
152 Mr. Jesse Fletcher
    Miss Ruth Fletcher
    Dr. Edward Hodges
    Mrs. Edward Hodges
162 Mr. N. J. Burford
    Mrs. N. J. Burford
    Wesley B. Burford
    Mr. John T. Burford
166 Mr. Wm. J. McKee
    Mrs. Wm. J. McKee
168 Mrs. Sara Richardson
182 Mr. Edward T. Claypool
    Mrs. Edward T. Claypool
200 Mr. Frederick Fahnley
    Mrs. Frederick Fahnley
    Miss Carrie Fahnley
    Miss Bertha Fahnley
    Mr. Henry Wetzel
    Mrs. Henry Wetzel
210 Mrs. Reginald H. Hall
    Mr. David R. Williams
224 Mr. Chas. H. Wood
    Mrs. Chas. H. Wood
237 Mr. E. B. Martindale
    Mrs. E. B. Martindale

237 Miss Emma Martindale
    Mr. Lynn Martindale
241 Mr. Henry W. Bennett
    Mrs. Henry W. Bennett
    Mr. Wm. Holliday
    Mrs. Wm. Holliday
247 Mr. Jas. W. Morris
    Mrs. Jas. W. Morris
    Miss Amelia W. Platter
250 Mr. Allen Fletcher
    Mrs. Allen Fletcher
    Miss Mary Fletcher
251 Mr. Wm. L. Barkley
    Mrs. Wm. L. Barkley
    Merrill B. Barkley
    Douglas J. Barkley
252 Mrs. Alfred Harrison
262 Mr. George W. Stout
    Mrs. George W. Stout
    Mr. Benj. F. Stout
271 Rev. John P. McCabe
    Mrs. John P. McCabe
275 Mrs. N. Morris
    Miss Kittie Morris
279 Mr. Walter Swiggett
    Mrs. Walter Swiggett
280 Mr. Wm. H. Brown
    Mrs. Wm. H. Brown
293 Mr. Granville Ballard
    Mrs. Granville Ballard
    Miss Lucile Ballard
294 Mr. D. L. Whittier
    Mrs. D. L. Whittier
    Miss A. G. Whittier

MERIDIAN STREET, NORTH.—Continued.

296 Mr. Allan Hendricks
 Mr. Ezra R. Hendricks
 Miss Caroline B. Hendricks
 Miss Bessie Hendricks
 Mrs. Laura B. Hendricks
297 Mr. Atwater Treat, Jr.
 Mrs. Atwater Treat, Jr.
 Mr. Edward L. Treat
315 Mr. Sam. Bufkin
 Mrs. Sam. Bufkin
 Miss Pearl Bufkin
316 Henry Bates, Jr.
 Mrs. Henry Bates, Jr.
 Mr. Chas. Martindale
 Mrs. Chas. Martindale
326 Mr. George Anthony
330 Mr. Austin Brown
 Mrs. Austin Brown
340 Mr. Owen R. Bailey
 Miss Frances A. Harper
 Mrs. Livingston Howland
 Capt. Wm. Mann
 Mrs. Wm. Mann
 Mrs. Rebecca Tyler
356 Mr. Wm. H. Tennis
 Mrs. Wm. H. Tennis
 Mr. Alva R. Tennis
358 Judge Wilson Morrow
 Mrs. Wilson Morrow
378 Mr. James Somerville
 Mrs. James Somerville
 Alfred H. Somerville
 James Somerville
 Miss Alice L. Somerville
 Mr. John Murray Somerville

382 Mr. Wm. B. Overman
 Mrs. Wm. B. Overman
400 Mr. John J. Cooper
 Mrs. John J. Cooper
 Mr. Chas. M. Cooper
 Mr. Earl Ogle
 Mrs. Earl Ogle
414 Mr. Geo. R. Sullivan
 Mrs. Geo. R. Sullivan
415 Mr. P. H. Fitzgerald
 Mrs. P. H. Fitzgerald
 Miss Laura Fitzgerald
 Mr. Frank Fitzgerald
 Mr. Philander H. Fitzgerald
421 Jesse H. Brown
 Herbert H. Brown
422 Mr. Terry J. Cullen
 Mrs. Terry J. Cullen
424 Miss Blanche Cole
427 Lynn P. Hollowell
438 Mrs. Ellen Catherwood
 Miss Mary Catherwood
440 Mr. Silas Baldwin
 Mrs. Silas Baldwin
 Mrs. W. S. Webb
 Mr. Courtland D. Webb
 Mrs. Courtland D. Webb
448 Mr. Wm. J. Brown
 Mrs. Wm. J. Brown
 Mr. John H. Ohr
 Mrs. John H. Ohr
466 Mrs. J. H. Wilson
 Mr. Bernard McGettigan
 Mr. John E. McGettigan

MERIDIAN STREET, NORTH.—Continued.

469	Mr. Wm. D. Hooper	528	Miss Catharine Lewis
	Mrs. Wm. D. Hooper		Mr. Chas. Allan Lewis
475	Rev. Wm. F. Taylor	545	Mr. Thos. Burdsal
	Mrs. Wm. F. Taylor		Mrs. Thos. Burdsal
480	Mr. Alexander M. Robertson		Miss Olive Burdsal
	Mrs. Alexander Robertson	546	Mr. Joseph J. Bingham
	Mr. Henry Weed		Mrs. Joseph J. Bingham
	Mrs. Henry Weed		Mr. F. L. Bingham
490	Mr. Augustus Kiefer		Mr. Edmund Bingham
	Mrs. Augustus Kiefer		Miss Emily S. Bingham
493	Mrs. Kate Moore Bowles		Miss Laura M. Bingham
	Mr. Joseph Bowles		Miss Emily Upfold
	Mr. Duane Bowles	548	Mr. George T. Evans
	Mr. Osborne Bowles		Mrs. George T. Evans
496	Mr. John F. Wallick		Mr. Edgar H. Evans
	Mrs. John F. Wallick	551	Mr. R. R. Shiel
	Mr. John Glenn Wallick		Mrs. R. R. Shiel
	Mary Glenn Wallick	553	Mr. Thomas Barry
	Miss Adele Wallick		Mrs. Thomas Barry
	Miss Katharine P. Wallick	564	Mr. Wm. K. Bellis
	Mr. Martin H. Wallick		Mrs. Wm. K. Bellis
505	Mr. Louis Hollweg		Mr. Chalmers Brown
	Mrs. Louis Hollweg	570	Mr. Roberts
	Miss Norma Hollweg		Mrs. Roberts
512	Mr. Charles E. Dark	573	Mr. Henry Severin
	Mrs. Charles E. Dark		Mrs. Henry Severin
	Mr. Edward Dark	600	Mr. David McCulloch
	Mr. Wilbur Dark		Mr. Carleton B. McCulloch
519	Miss Agnes Finch	611	Mrs. Eliza S. Hendricks
	Mr. John Moore		Miss Anna B. Hendricks
	Mrs. John Moore		Mr. Victor R. Hendricks
	Mr. Arthur C. Moore		Mrs. Victor R. Hendricks
526	Mr. Wm. C. Hall	616	Mr. Wm. S. Hubbard
	Mrs. Wm. C. Hall	617	Mrs. G. Maxwell
528	Mrs. Catharine Lewis		Marion Maxwell

THE ELITE LIST.

MERIDIAN STREET, NORTH.—Continued.

617 Miss Georgia Maxwell
620 Mrs. Harriet R. Dean
　　Mr. Stewart Dean
　　Miss Mary Dean
　　Miss Wilfred Dean
621 Mr. Henry L. Van Hoff
　　Mrs. Henry L. Van Hoff
　　Miss Van Valkenburg
622 Mr. Henry Knippenberg
　　Mrs. Henry Knippenberg
　　Miss Knippenberg
625 Mr. Arthur D. Jaillet
　　Mrs. Arthur D. Jaillet
627 Mr. Charles L. Lawrence
　　Mr. Mason J. Osgood
　　Mrs. Mason J. Osgood
629 Mr. Fernandez Simmonds
　　Mrs. Fernandez Simmonds
　　Miss Nellie E. Simmonds
　　Miss Blanche A. Simmonds
635 Mr. George C. Beck
　　Mrs. George C. Beck
　　Miss Bessie Beck
　　Mr. George A. Beck
654 Mr. Robert B. F. Pierce
　　Mrs. Robert B. F. Pierce
　　Mr. Edward Pierce
660 Mr. John Newman Carey
　　Mrs. John Newman Carey
661 Mr. Edward Charles Egan
　　Mrs. Edward Charles Egan
　　Mr. Pirtle Herod
　　Mrs. Pirtle Herod
663 Mr. Joseph B. Mansur
　　Mrs. Joseph B. Mansur

670 Mr. Fred. M. Buchanan
　　Mrs. Fred. M. Buchanan
　　Dr. Calvin I. Fletcher
673 Mr. Wm. C. Brazington
699 Mr. Fred. Winters
　　Mrs. Fred. Winters
　　Miss Kate Winters
　　Miss Sue Winters
　　Mr. Thomas Winters
700 Mr. W. B. Burford
　　Mrs. W. B. Burford
　　Mr. Wm. B. Bradford
　　Mrs. Wm. B. Bradford
　　Mrs. Wm. Henderson
　　Mrs. Joseph P. Wiggins
　　Mr. Dudley H. Wiggins
712 Mr. Clarence Wulsen
　　Mrs. Clarence Wulsen
725 Mr. Henry D. Pierce
　　Mrs. Henry D. Pierce
　　Miss Elizabeth Pierce
729 Mr. Arthur Jordan
　　Mrs. Arthur Jordan
731 Mr. Wm. Herod
　　Mrs. Wm. Herod
　　Miss Lucy Herod
　　Mr. Joseph Herod
733 Mr. Isaac Thalman
　　Mrs. Isaac Thalman
735 Mrs. John H. Stewart
　　Miss Kate G. Stewart
744 Mr. Addison C. Harris
　　Mrs. Addison C. Harris
750 Mr. John Thomas

MERIDIAN STREET, NORTH.—Continued.

775	Mr. Victor Bachus	830	Miss Evans A. Ensley
	Mrs. Victor Bachus		Mr. Oscar J. Ensley
776	Mr. Chas. Mayer	832	Mr. Geo. R. Randolph
	Mrs. Chas. Mayer		Mrs. Geo. R. Randolph
777	Mr. Daniel Fred. Appel		Mr. W. R. Randolph
	Mrs. Daniel Fred. Appel		Mr. Parker Randolph
781	Mrs. Jane Galbraith	834	Mr. Lewis Levey
	Miss Harriet Galbraith		Mrs. Lewis Levey
790	Mr. Albert S. Comstock	836	Mr. Henry Malpas
	Mrs. Albert S. Comstock		Mrs. Henry Malpas
800	Mr. Alonzo P. Hendrickson		Mr. Samuel Malpas
	Mrs. Alonzo P. Hendrickson		Mr. Charles E. Malpas
	Miss Pearl Kaufman	837	Mr. Byron K. Elliot
805	Mrs. Eliza J. Jones		Mrs. Byron K. Elliott
	Miss Fannie Jones		Mr. Wm. Frederick Elliot
809	Mr. John Whitut	853	Mr. Henry Eitle
	Mrs. John Whitut		Mrs. Henry Eitle
810	Mrs. James L. Fletcher	854	Mr. David W. Coffin
815	Dr. F. W. Rose		Mrs. David W. Coffin
	Mrs. F. W. Rose		Miss Florence North Coffin
	Mr. George K. Trask	855	Mr. Howard Benton
	Mrs. George K. Trask		Mrs. Howard Benton
820	Mr. T. C. Day	857	Mr. Hugh M. Green
	Mrs. T. C. Day		Mrs. Hugh M. Green
	Mrs. Florence Day	860	Mr. John M. Maxwell
825	Mr. James L. Fugate		Mrs. John M. Maxwell
	Mrs. James L. Fugate	861	Mr. J. M. Adsit
	Miss Fannie Fugate	862	Mr. Chas. K. Mavity
826	Mr. Alfred D. Gates		Mrs. Chas. K. Mavity
	Mrs. Alfred D. Gates		Dr. L. C. Cline
	Mr. Edward Gates		Mrs. L. C. Cline
	Mr. Hewitt H. Howland	863	Dr. Wm. S. Beck
	Mrs. Hewitt H. Howland		Mrs. Wm. S. Beck
830	Mr. Nicholas Ensley		Harry Abraham Beck
	Mrs. Nicholas Ensley		

MERIDIAN STREET, NORTH.—Continued.

926 Mr. Thos. B. Jackson
    Mrs. Thos. B. Jackson
928 Mr. Thos. Moorehead
    Mrs. Thos. Moorehead
    Mr. Robert Moorehead
    Miss Maud Moorehead
930 Mr. Chas. H. Swiggett
    Mrs. Chas. H. Swiggett
932 Mr. Noah W. Kumler
    Mrs. Noah W. Kumler
935 Fred. A. Gregory
    Mrs. Fred. A. Gregory
    Mrs. Martha M. Gregory
937 Mr. Phillip M. Hildebrand
    Mrs. Phillip M. Hildebrand
940 Mr. John Stevenson
    Mrs. John Stevenson
942 Mr. Laban Lycurgus Goode
    Mrs. Laban Lycurgus Goode
    Miss Vinnie R. Goode
    Mr. Charles Norton Goode
950 Mr. Wm. W. Winslow
    Mrs. Wm. W. Winslow
952 Mr. Gustave Recker
    Mrs. Gustave Recker
    Mr. Newall Rogers
954 Mr. Lewis H. McMurray
    Mrs. Lewis H. McMurray
956 Mr. Benj. B. Minor
    Mrs. Benj. B. Minor
    Miss Eugene V. Minor
    Miss Gertrude Minor
958 Mr. Joseph Rink
    Mrs. Joseph Rink
975 Albert S. Blackledge

975 John W. Blackledge
    Susan K. Blackledge
    Irene L. Blackledge
984 Mr. Frederick Francke
    Mrs. Frederick Francke
985 Mr. James McCullough
    Mrs. James McCullough
994 Rev. J. A. Roundthaler
    Mrs. J. A. Roundthaler
    Miss Marion Roundthaler
    Miss Ethiel Roundthaler
    Mr. Robert Roundthaler
1000 Mr. John S. Lazarus
    Mrs. John S. Lazarus
    Mr. George M. Lazarus
1022 Mr. John Clune
    Mrs. John Clune
    Miss Clune
1024 Judge George L. Reinhard
    Mrs. George L. Reinhard
    Miss Anna Reinhard
1026 Mr. Derk DeRinter
    Mrs. Derk DeRinter
1028 Mr. Ansen J. Gardner
    Mrs. nsen J. Gardner
1108 Mr. John C. Pierson
    Mrs. John C. Pierson
    Mr. Ernst Pierson
1134 Mr. Lynn Milliken
    Mrs. Lynn Milliken
1667 Mr. Frederick Webster
    Mrs. Frederick Webster
1691 Mr. Joseph G. McDowell
    Mrs. Joseph G. McDowell

MICHIGAN STREET, EAST.

10	Mrs. Margaret Staats	100	Miss Hasselman
	Mrs. T. Martin Staats	117	Miss Jessie E. Malock
12	Rev. John H. Ranger		Mr. John H. Murphy
	Mrs. John H. Ranger		Mrs. John H. Murphy
16	Mr. Wm. Line Elder	119	Mr. Geo. F. Branham
	Mrs. Wm. Line Elder		Mrs. Geo. F. Branham
76	Mr. Harold B. Eldridge		Geo. E. Branham
	Mr. Wm. J. Eldridge	124	Mr. Edward B. Porter
83	Miss Marie Woolpert		Mrs. Edward B. Porter
84	Mr. Geo. B. Yandes	194	Dr. Hugo Pantzer
	Mrs. Elizabeth Y. Robinson		Mrs. Hugo Pantzer
	Mr. Joseph R. Robinson	215	Mr. Augustus B. Kern
100	Mr. Otto H. Hasselman		Mrs. Augustus B. Kern
	Mrs. Otto H. Hasselman	274	Chas. E. Hunt

MICHIGAN STREET, WEST.

16	Mr. Joseph B. Warne	122	Mr. Robert S. Sinclair
	Mrs. Joseph B. Warne	139	Mr. A. Judson Smith
74	Mr. Morris M. Defrees		Mrs. A. Judson Smith
	Mrs. Morris M. Defrees	567	Mr. Chas. C. Williams
	Mr. Fred. Defrees		Mrs. Chas. C. Williams
78	Mr. Chas. Schurman		
	Mrs. Chas. Schurman		

MIDDLE DRIVE, (W. P.)

63	Mr. Chas. S. Bronson	81	Mrs. Milton S. Huey
	Mrs. Chas. S. Bronson		Miss Laura Huey
78	Dr. Maurice Albrecht	107	Mr. Chauncy Butler
	Mrs. Maurice Albrecht		Mrs. Chauncy Butler
81	Mr. Milton S. Huey		Miss Bessie Butler

MISSISSIPPI STREET, NORTH.

276 Mr. Flavius J. Van Vorhis
Mrs. Flavius J. Van Vorhis
401 Mr. Henry W. Interviler
Mrs. Henry W. Interviler
Mr. Henry W. Interviler, Jr.
577 Mr. George W. Atkins
Mrs. George W. Atkins
611 Mr. Wm. H. Laycock
998 Mr. Adolph Schleicher
Mrs. Adolph Schleicher

MORRISON STREET.

11 Mr. John D. Holliday
Mrs. John D. Holliday
Mr. Wm. Warren Holliday
Edward J. Holliday
21 Mr. Edwin M. Goodwin
Mrs. Edwin M. Goodwin
21 Mrs. Eliza P. Newcomb
28 Mr. Chauncey R. Watren
Mrs. Chauncey R. Watren
29 Mr. Wm. Holton Dye
Mrs. Wm. Holton Dye

NEW JERSEY STREET, NORTH.

162 Mr. Lorenz Schmidt
Mrs. Lorenz Schmidt
169 Dr. Allison Maxwell
Mrs. Allison Maxwell
175 Mr. Henry S. Hanckel
Mrs. Henry S. Hanckel
181 Dr. Graham A. Wells
Mrs. Graham A. Wells
186 Mr. Glenn Howe
Mrs. Glenn Howe
221 Mr. Chas. W. Wells
Mrs. Chas. W. Wells
Mr. Livingston D. Wells
280 Mr. Wm. Daggett
Mrs. Wm. Daggett
Miss Cora Olive Daggett
290 Mr. James B. Ryan
Mrs. James B. Ryan
293 Rev. Daniel R. Lucas
Mrs. Daniel R. Lucas
Miss Catharine Lucas
Miss Maud E. Lucas
321 Mr. Michael Sells
Mrs. Michael Sells
Corwin Sells
331 Miss Nellie Ahern
352 Mr. Robert S. Foster
Mrs. Robert S. Foster
Mr. Clarence M. Foster
Miss Rose Foster
399 Miss Prudence E. Lewis
439 Mr. Frank X. Arms
Mrs. Frank X. Arms
855½ Mr. Conrad Schellschmidt
Mrs. Conrad Schellschmidt

NEW YORK STREET, EAST.

121	Mr. Henry Coburn	220	Mr. Ralph Hill
	Mrs. Henry Coburn		Mrs. Ralph Hill
	Mr. Wm. H. Coburn		Ralph Hill, Jr.
	Mrs. Wm. H. Coburn	271	Mr. James Broden
	Henry Coburn, Jr.		Mrs. James Broden
148	Mr. George F. Adams		James Broden, Jr.
	Mrs. George F. Adams	277	Mr. Wm. A. Peele, Jr.
	Miss Lida Adams		Mrs. Wm. A. Peele, Jr.

OHIO STREET, EAST.

19	Dr. Franklin Hays	180	Mr. Stoughton J. Fletcher
	Mrs. Franklin Hays	246	Mr. Adolph Schellschmidt
	Miss Mary Patterson		Miss Emma Schellschmidt

OHIO STREET, WEST.

73	Mr. Wm. C. Thompson	134	Wm. C. Esterbrook
	Mrs. Wm. C. Thompson		Guy R. Esterbrook

PARK AVENUE.

37	Francis M. Crouse	200	Amand M. Lee
	Miss Jeanette Crouse		Anna Blanche Lee
116	Mrs. Anna B. Dearborn	210	Mr. Noble C. Butler
	Miss Dearborn		Mrs. Noble C. Butler
	Mr. Clair S. Dearborn		Miss Mary Browning Butler
160	Mr. Joel W. Hadley		Mr. John A. Butler
	Mrs. Joel W. Hadley	211	Mrs. Elizabeth Brown Adams
	Miss Margaret Hamilton		Miss Edith Adams
172	Mr. Nathan H. Kipp		Miss Kate Adams
	Mrs. Nathan H. Kipp		Henry Alden Adams
183	Mr. John W. Dalrymple	223	Mr. Geo. W. Hufford
	Mrs. John W. Dalrymple		Mrs. Geo. W. Hufford
	Miss Helen Dalrymple		

PARK AVENUE.—Continued.

235 Mr. Wm. D. Seaton
Mrs. Wm. D. Seaton
Miss Helen Seaton
Mr. Wm. Seaton
Mr. Albert Seaton
Mr. Howland Seaton
Mr. Clark Seaton
247 Mr. Fabias M. Finch
Mrs. Fabias M. Finch
Mr. John A. Finch
Miss Alice Finch
268 Mr. John M. Shaw
Mrs. John M. Shaw
291 Mr. Wm. Thos. Brown
Mrs. Wm. Thos. Brown
298 Miss Henrietta Colgan
Miss Mary Colgan
Dr. Albert C. Reinberlin
Mrs. Albert C. Reinberlin
Mr. Chas. S. Roney
Mrs. Chas. S. Roney
300 Mr. John B. Elam
Mrs. John B. Elam
311 Mrs. Harriet B. Hall
Mr. Arthur F. Hall
Miss Emma Hall
315 Mr. James McAlpin
Mrs. James McAlpin
320 Mr. Matthew Cummings
Mrs. Matthew Cummings
329 Mr. Wm. A. Hughes
Mrs. Wm. A. Hughes
Miss Jessie Hughes
332 Mr. Edwin S. Folsom
Mrs. Edwin S. Folsom
Miss Mabel Folsom

345 Mr. John C. Ingram
Mrs. John C. Ingram
350 Mrs. Charlotte Baker
Miss Alice Baker
358 Mr. Carl Von Hake
Mrs. Carl Von Hake
360 Mr. John B. Conner
Mrs. John B. Conner
Miss Adah Conner
364 Mr. John Budd
Mrs. John Budd
367 Dr. Jesse D. George
Mrs. Jesse D. George
370 Mr. Braxton Baker
Mrs. Braxton Baker
374 Mr. Harry Murphy
Mrs. Harry Murphy
380 Mr. Allen Conduit
Mrs. Allen Conduit
Miss Mabel Conduit
383 Mr. Edward S. Sequin
Mrs. Edward S. Sequin
384 Mr. Alexander Taggart
Mrs. Alexander Taggart
388 Mr. George H. Behm
Mrs. George H. Behm
393 Mr. Albert W. Coffin
Mrs. Albert W. Coffin
395 Dr. Hugh Lash
Mrs. Hugh Lash
410 Mr. Charles W. Fairbanks
Mrs. Charles W. Fairbanks
Miss Adelaide Fairbanks
422 Mr. Henry Clay Roney
Mrs. Henry Clay Roney

THE ELITE LIST.

PARK AVENUE.—Continued.

440 Mr. Arthur H. Webb
     Mrs. Arthur H. Webb
446 Mrs. Drusilla Wilson
453 Mr. John M. Paver
     Mrs. John M. Paver
     Miss Augusta Paver
     Mr. John Paver
474 Mr. Joseph H. Stubbs
     Mrs. Joseph H. Stubbs

477 Mr. John L. McMaster
     Mrs. John L. McMaster
     Miss Edith McMaster
579 Mr. Michael W. Carr
     Mrs. Michael W. Carr
598 Mr. Charles A. Nicholi
     Mrs. Charles A. Nicholi

PENNSYLVANIA ST., NORTH.

122 Rev. Henry Day
     Mr. Henry McCarty Day
     Miss Margaret Day
     Mr. Nicholas McCarty
     Miss Fannie J. McCarty
129 Mrs. Anna Dorland
130 Dr. Isaac C. Walker
     Mrs. Isaac C. Walker
143 P. G. C. Hunt
145 Dr. John M. Kitchen
     Mrs. John M. Kitchen
147 Mrs. M. S. Wallace
163 Mr. John S. Spann
     Mrs. John S. Spann
     Mr. Henry Spann
179 Mr. Hervey Vories
     Mrs. Hervey Vories
199 Mr. Geo. E. Hunt
     Mr. Wm. Harper Morrison
     Mrs. Wm. Harper Morrison
201 Mr. S. B. Dudbridge
     Mrs. S. B. Dudbridge

203 Mr. John H. Dilks
     Agnes Hyland Dilks
     Nellie Eleanor Dilks
209 Mr. Furnam Stout
     Mrs. Furnam Stout
229 Mr. Jacob G. Hollenbeck
     Mrs. Jacob G. Hollenbeck
     Mr. David Parmelee
     Mrs. David Parmelee
230 Mr. Wm. Houston Talbott
     Mrs. E. C. Talbott
239 Mr. John W. Murphy
     Mrs. John W. Murphy
240 Miss Margareta Stevens
248 Miss M. G. Sprague
272 Mr. Frank A. Blanchard
     Mrs. Frank A. Blanchard
     Hon. John C. New
     Mrs. John C. New
     Miss Elizabeth R. New
275 Mr. Horatio Newcombe
     Mrs. Horatio Newcombe

PENNSYLVANIA STREET, NORTH. Continued.

275 Col. John W. Ray
Mrs. John W. Ray
Miss Elizabeth Ray
Miss Lucia Holliday Ray
282 Reed Carr
Mr. Max Leckener
Mrs. Max Leckener
288 Miss Winnifred Jackson
Mr. George McCurdy
Mrs. George McCurdy
Miss Halcyone McCurdy
Mr. Wm. Isaac McCurdy
297 Dr. Quincy Van Hummel
Mrs. Quincy Van Hummel
Dr. Henry Van Hummel
321 Mr. Theodore Krauss
Mrs. Theodore Krauss
331 Mrs. Elizabeth R. Dickinson
Alice E. Dickinson
Jennie E. Dickinson
335 Mrs. Margaret Dietrich
Miss Nettie Dietrich
339 Mr. Edgar J. Foster
Mrs. Edgar J. Foster
Miss Florence Day Foster
Miss Sarah W. Foster
Miss Frances H. Foster
343 Mr. Theodore Lovett Sewell
Mrs. Mary W. Sewell
345 Mrs. M. F. Sproule
Miss Anna Sproule
359 Mrs. Margaret Ayler
385 Mr. James H. Baldwin
Mrs. James H. Baldwin
Miss Margaret Baldwin

391 Mr. Wm. Gustave Krauss
Mrs. Wm. Gustave Krauss
393 Mr. Chas. Krauss
Mrs. Chas. Krauss
397 Rev. Mathias L. Haines
Mrs. Mathias L. Haines
399 Judge James Black
Mrs. James Black
401 Mr. Upton J. Hammond
Mrs. Upton J. Hammond
402 Miss Julia Ethel Landers
Miss Pearl Landers
409 Miss Laura Meigs
Miss Mary Meigs
410 Mr. Wm. C. Smith
Mrs. Wm. C. Smith
Anna T. Smith
415 Mr. James A. Wildman
Mrs. James A. Wildman
Miss Anna Wildman
417 Mr. Daniel L. Wood
Mrs. Daniel L. Wood
Mr. Willis G. Wood
Mr. Herbert S. Wood
Mr. Edson L. Wood
Miss Marcia M. Wood
422 Mr. Hanford A. Edson
Mrs. Hanford A. Edson
429 Mr. Howard Albert Dill
Mrs. Howard Albert Dill
433 Mr. James Lodge
Mrs. James Lodge
439 Mr. Robert W. Cathcart
Mrs. Robert W. Cathcart

PENNSYLVANIA STREET, NORTH.—Continued.

453	Mr. E. N. Richards	494	Alice Graydon
	Mrs. E. N. Richards		Mr. Alexander Graydon
	Miss Nellie Richards	500	Mr. Marcus L. Hare
457	Mr. Isaac L. Bloomer		Mrs. Marcus L. Hare
	Mrs. Isaac L. Bloomer		Mr. Clinton L. Hare
	Asahel Bloomer		Mrs. Clinton L. Hare
462	Mr. Chas. Bundy	515	Mr. John E. Bradshaw
	Mr. Albert Johnson	519	Mr. Edwin Nichols
	Mr. Chas. Wm. Medearis		Mrs. Edwin Nichols
	Mr. Fletcher C. Medearis		Mr. Benj. O. Nichols
	John M. Stern	562	Mrs. Abbie Mayo
463	Mr. Joseph E. Taylor		Miss Lucy Mayo
	Mrs. Joseph E. Taylor		Miss Henrietta Mayo
	George Bryan Taylor		Miss Anna Mayo
466	Mrs. Maria Finch		Miss Sadie Mayo
	Mr. Frank W. Morrison	564	Mr. David Cox
467	Mr. Jacob Piatt Dunn		Mrs. David Cox
	Mrs. Jacob Piatt Dunn	566	Mr. Jerome G. Whitcomb
	Mrs. Flora C. Jones		Mrs. Jerome G. Whitcomb
471	Mr. C. S. Phillips		Miss Nellie C. Whitcomb
	Miss Grace Phillips		Mr. George E. Whitcomb
	Miss Kate Phillips	575	Mr. Henry Schurman
474	Mr. Wm. C. Dickson		Mrs. Henry Schurman
	Mrs. Wm. C. Dickson	578	Mr. Horace Smith
	Miss Emma Dickson		Mrs. Horace Smith
477	Mrs. Frances M. Farquhar		Mr. John R. Pearson
	Miss Anna Farquhar		Mrs. John R. Pearson
	Miss Caroline Farquhar	582	Mr. Vinson Carter
	Mrs. Eliza G. Wiley		Mrs. Vinson Carter
478	Mr. Wm. C. MacCurdy		Miss Anna Louise Carter
	Mrs. Wm. C. MacCurdy		Miss Elizabeth Hughes
481	Mr. John W. Kern	593	Mr. Addison L. Roache
	Mrs. John W. Kern		Mrs. Addison L. Roache
494	Mr. Andrew Graydon		Miss Belle W. Roache
	Mrs. Andrew Graydon		Jamie E. Roache

PENNSYLVANIA STREET, NORTH.— Continued.

- 596 Llewellyn Blanton
- 597 Mr. Wm. R. Silvester
  - Mrs. Wm. R. Silvester
  - Mr. Wm. B. Silvester
- 598 Mr. John S. Tarkington
  - Mrs. John S. Tarkington
  - Mr. Booth Tarkington
- 599 Mr. Thomas Bassett
  - Mrs. Thomas Bassett
  - Miss Ella M. Waite
- 600 Mr. Ward Hunt Dean
  - Mrs. Ward Hunt Dean
- 610 Mr. Henry Clay Long
  - Mrs. Henry Clay Long
- 615 Mrs. Ferdinandina Reese
  - Miss Lillie Reese
  - Mr. Louis Chas. Reese
- 619 Mr. Michael Clune
  - Mrs. Michael Clune
  - Miss Anna Clune
  - Mr. Wm. J. Clune
- 621 Mr. Joshua G. Frazer
  - Mrs. Joshua G. Frazer
  - Miss Elizabeth Frazer
- 622 Mr. Wm. F. Landers
  - Mr. Jackson Landers
  - Mrs. Jackson Landers
  - Miss Lillie B. Landers
- 625 Mr. Addison Bybee
  - Mrs. Addison Bybee
  - Miss Jessie Bybee
  - Miss Alice Bybee
- 626 Mr. Samuel A. Johnston
  - Mrs. Samuel A. Johnston
  - Mrs. Eliza A. Pullis

- 627 Mrs. J. D. Howland
  - Miss Caroline H. Howland
- 630 Mr. J. C. Ferree
  - Mrs. J. C. Ferree
- 640 Mrs. Catharine E. Ruschaupt
- 644 Mr. Geo. A. Dickson
  - Mrs. Geo. A. Dickson
  - Mr. John L. Dickson
  - Mrs. John L. Dickson
- 651 Mr. Benj. B. Peck
  - Mrs. Benj. B. Peck
- 653 Mr. Alexander E. Wells
  - Miss Eleanor S. Wells
  - Miss Margaret Wells
- 661 Ex.-Gov. Isaac P. Gray
  - Mrs. Isaac P. Gray
  - Mr. Pierce Gray
  - Mrs. Pierce Gray
- 670 Mrs. B. F. Hough
  - Miss Ida Hough
- 673 Mr. Caleb S. Denny
  - Mrs. Caleb S. Denny
  - Miss Mary Denny
  - Miss Carrie Denny
- 675 Mr. Josiah K. Lilly
  - Mrs. Josiah K. Lilly
- 704 Mrs. Rebecca J. Stevenson
  - Miss Margaret Stevenson
  - Mr. Benj. Stevenson
- 705 Mr. Harry E. Drew
  - Mrs. Harry E. Drew
- 735 Mrs. Anna Boggs
- 737 Mr. Ovid B. Jameson
  - Mrs. Ovid B. Jameson

PENNSYLVANIA STREET, NORTH.—Continued.

738 Mr. George Carleton
Mrs. Fannie Carleton
749 Mr. Henry L. Wallace
Mrs. Henry L. Wallace
755 Mr. Alfred Ogle
Mrs. Alfred Ogle
759 Mr. Winifred Miller
Mrs. Winifred Miller
762 Mr. Thos. MacIntire
Mrs. Thos. MacIntire
Miss Mary MacIntire
Mr. Chapin Clark Foster
Mrs. Chapin Clark Foster
765 Mr. Horace S. Bennett
766 Mr. Chas. Jenkins
Mrs. Chas. Jenkins
768 Mr. Ovid Butler
Mrs. Ovid Butler
770 Mr. Merrick E. Vinton
Mrs. Merrick E. Vinton
Mr. Thos. M. Vinton
772 Mr. Geo. Herman West
Mrs. Geo. Herman West
Miss Bessie Marie West
777 Mr. Benj. D. Walcott
Mrs. Benj. D. Walcott
778 Mr. James Raynor Lilly
Mrs. James Raynor Lilly
784 Mr. W. S. Garber
Mrs. W. S. Garber
785 Miss Caldwell
Mr. Benjamin Jones
Mrs. Benjamin Jones
786 Mr. Henry Hanna
Mrs. Henry Hanna
Mrs. Mary S. Moore

786 Miss Julia Moore
Miss Deborah Moore
789 Mr. Louis G. Deschler
Mrs. Louis G. Deschler
790 Dr. Francis J. Hammond
Mrs. Francis J. Hammond
Miss Katharine Stone
800 Mr. Chas. E. Coffin
Mrs. Chas. E. Coffin
820 Mr. Daniel Winings
Mrs. Daniel Winings
826 Mr. Ernest R. Keith
Mrs. Ernest R. Keith
828 Mr. Wm. Watson Woolen
Mrs. Wm. Watson Woolen
Miss Marie Woolen
Mr. Evans Woolen
Mr. Harry Woolen
830 Mr. Louis H. Gibson
Mrs. Louis H. Gibson
831 Mr. John F. Carson
Mrs. John F. Carson
Mr. Edward Carson
832 Miss Fredonia Allen
Miss Mary Grubb
Miss Jane Grubb
844 Mr. Chas. E. Holloway
Mrs. Chas. E. Holloway
846 Mr. John O. Henderson
Mrs. John O. Henderson
848 Mr. Horace F. Wood
Mrs. Horace F. Wood
850 Mrs. Thos. Sharpe
Miss Belle Sharpe
851 Mr. Macy Malott
Mrs. Macy Malott

PENNSYLVANIA STREET, NORTH.—Continued.

853	Mr. Chas. L. Liebert	884	Mr. Frank Talbott
	Mrs. Chas. L. Liebert		Mrs. Frank Talbott
854	Mr. Edmund Gall	886	Mrs. F. S. Newcomer
	Mrs. Edmund Gall		Miss Newcomer
858	Mrs. Ada Duzan	887	Mr. Augustus Coburn
859	Mr. Wm. R. Brown		Mrs. Augustus Coburn
	Mrs. Wm. R. Brown	939	Mr. Wm. Hunter
864	Mrs. Martha Ridenour		Mrs. Wm. Hunter
	Emma B. Ridenour		Ellis F. Hunter
866	Miss Lina Baris	947	Mr. Chas. Eli Hall
	Rev. Willis D. Engle		Mrs. Chas. Eli Hall
	Mrs. Willis D. Engle	950	Mr. Albert Edw. Buchanan
	Mr. John Wainright		Mrs. Albert Edw. Buchanan
	Mrs. John Wainright	953	Mr. Edward J. Robinson
868	Miss Eliza Ford		Mrs. Edward J. Robinson
	Miss Belle Ford	954	Mr. Alexander Spenance
870	Mr. George Talbott		Mrs. Alexander Spenance
	Mrs. George Talbott	975	Maj. Wm. A. Richards
874	Mr. Chas. Thompson		Mrs. W. A. Richards
	Mrs. Chas. Thompson		Mr. Hugh R. Richards
875	Mr. Benjamin Hitz	1020	Mr. John R. Lowe
	Mrs. Benjamin Hitz		Mrs. John R. Lowe
880	Mr. David Swan		Miss Lena Alice Lowe
	Mrs. David Swan		Miss Winnie A. Lowe
	Miss Edna Swan	1024	Mr. Walter F. C. Golt
883	Mr. Edward Daniels		Mrs. Walter F. C. Golt
	Mrs. Edward Daniels	1091	Mr. Frank C. Payne
			Mrs. Frank C. Payne

PRATT STREET, EAST.

20 Miss Eliza Benton
    Mrs. Corene T. Browning
    Miss Anna Nicholas
    Mr. Martin Taylor Ohr
    Mrs. Martin Taylor Ohr
79 Mr. Chas. W. Smith
    Mrs. Chas. W. Smith
    Miss Grace Smith
    Margaret E. Smith
    Albert P. Smith
86 Miss Rhoda E. Selleck
116 Mr. George Geiger
    Mrs. George Geiger
    Mr. John L. Geiger

118 Mr. John E. Smith
    Mrs. John E. Smith
    Mr. Harold O. Smith
    Miss Kate May Smith
    Miss Josephine Smith
122 Mr. Wm. Fred. Stiltz
    Mrs. Wm. Fred. Stiltz
137 Mr. John E. Christian
    Mrs. John E. Christian
141 Mr. Wm. S. Fish
    Mrs. Wm. S. Fish
    Miss Julia Fish
    Miss Mary E. Fish
    Mr. Wm. Ross Fish

RUCKLE STREET.

53 Mr. Richard Lew Dawson
    Mrs. Levina Thompson
64 Mr. Ernest P. Bicknell
    Mrs. Ernest P. Bicknell

116 Mr. Edward C. Buskirk
    Mrs. Edward C. Buskirk

ST. CLAIR STREET, EAST.

168 Mr. Enoch Warman
    Mrs. Enoch Warman
    Miss Nancy Warman

309 Mr. Joseph Marott
    Mrs. Joseph Marott
311 Mr. Geo. J. Marott
    Mrs. Geo. J. Marott

ST. CLAIR STREET, WEST.

32 Mr. John E. Cleland
    Mrs. John E. Cleland
    Miss Harriet Cleland

ST. JOSEPH STREET, EAST.

73 Mr. Theo. A. Randall
   Mrs. Theo. A. Randall
75 Mrs. Deborah Moore
   Mr. Thos. Claxton Moore
   Miss Miriam Moore
   Louise Duane Moore
76 Mr. Walter C. Evans

127 Mr. Edward James Bain
    Mrs. Edward James Bain
    Miss Bessie Louise Bain
    Mr. Harry Clegg Bain
129 Mr. Coke Alexander
    Mrs. Coke Alexander
    Miss Bessie Wilkinson
200 Mrs. May Johnson

TALBOTT AVENUE.

62 Mr. Frank Wood
   Mrs. Frank Wood
64 Mr. Wm. Husbands
   Mrs. Wm. Husbands
66 Mr. Carl Swiggett
   Mrs. Carl Swiggett
71 Mr. Richard E. Chislett
   Mrs. Richard E. Chislett

109 Mr. James V. Stanbury
    Mrs. James V. Stanbury
110 Mrs. Chas. B. Coe
    Miss Anna May Coe
112 Rev. Chas. H. McDowell
    Mrs. Chas. H. McDowell
248 Mr. D. W. Edwards
    Mrs. D. W. Edwards

TENNESSEE STREET, NORTH.

126 Mrs. Barbara Donnan
    Miss Emma Donnan
    Miss Laura Donnan
    Mr. Theodore Donnan
181 Mr. Wm. H. Cooper
    Mrs. Wm. H. Cooper
    Mr. Wm. Cooper
196 Mr. Daniel A. Lemon
    Mrs. Daniel A. Lemon
    Miss Daisy Lemon

225 Mr. Henry Martin Bronson
    Mrs. Henry Martin Bronson
    Frank Ferris Bronson
227 Miss Katherine Merrill
240 Dr. E. J. Brennan
    Mrs. E. J. Brennan
    Vincent Graham Brennan
247 Mr. George L. Raschig
250 Mr. George G. Tanner
    Mrs. George G. Tanner
    Miss Maria Tanner

THE ELITE LIST.

TENNESSEE STREET, NORTH.—Continued.

253 Mr. Thos. L. Sullivan
Mrs. Thos. L. Sullivan
257 Miss Merrill
264 Mr. Alonzo G. Smith
Mrs. Alonzo G. Smith
265 Miss Lena Ingraham
273 Mr. Geo. O. Griffin
Mrs. Geo. O. Griffin
Mr. Michael S. Griffin
Mr. George G. Griffin
Miss Martha B. Griffin
Miss Brook Griffin
279 Mr. Elisha H. Hall
Mrs. Elisha H. Hall
Mr. Albert Fitch Hall
284 Mrs. Thomas Gibson
288 Mr. George C. Hitt
Mrs. George C. Hitt
294 Dr. Richard F. Stone
Mrs. Richard F. Stone
311 Mr. Otto Leiber
Mrs. Otto Leiber
333 Mr. Christian Brink
Miss Matilda Brink
Miss Louise C. Brink
340 Mr. Thomas Walker
Mrs. Thomas Walker
344 Mr. Samuel H. Fletcher
Mrs. Samuel H. Fletcher
Mr. Lafayette W. Fletcher
Mrs. Lafayette W. Fletcher
348 Mr. R. K. Syfers
Mrs. R. K. Syfers
351 Mr. Joshua S. Smith
Mrs. Joshua S. Smith
Miss Jeanette Smith

358 Mr. Wm. P. Gallup
366 Mr. George R. Share
Mrs. George R. Share
Louis Adsit Share
Mary Frances Share
373 Mr. Elmer C. Sewall
Mrs. Elmer C. Sewall
Miss Alice M. Sewall
381 Mr. Dewitt Nay
Mrs. Dewitt Nay
384 Mr. Chas. F. Wymond
Mrs. Chas. F. Wymond
Mr. John W. Bryant
Mrs. John W. Bryant
400 Mr. Wm. Coughlen
Mrs. Wm. Coughlen
Miss Mary Coughlen
Frank W. Coughlen
Mr. Wm. F. Coughlen
Dr. Edward Coughlen
410 Mr. Thos. Taggart
Mrs. Thos. Taggart
428 Mr. Ernst Wiles
Mrs. Ernst Wiles
437 Mr. Steven K. Fletcher
Mrs. Steven K. Fletcher
444 Mr. Fielding T. Lee
Mrs. Fielding T. Lee
449 Mr. Isaac Frankem
Mrs. Isaac Frankem
451 Mr. Frederick Bush
Mrs. Frederick Bush
454 Col. Eli Lilly
Mrs. Eli Lilly
455 Mr. George Bliss
Mrs. George Bliss

TENNESSEE STREET, NORTH. —Continued.

474 Mrs. Taylor
Miss Alice Taylor
477 Mr. Wm. S. Tarkington
Mrs. Wm. S. Tarkington
501 Hon. Albert G. Porter
512 Mrs. Eugenia McQuot
Miss Tolkerbie McQuot
545 Mr. Richard Schliewen
Mrs. Richard Schliewen
553 Mr. Jacob T. Southern
Mrs. Jacob T. Southern
560 Mr. Wm. Albert Bristoe
Mrs. Wm. Albert Bristoe
Miss Burton Bristoe
573 Mr. Thomas Dean
Mrs. Thomas Dean
Mr. John Kingsbury Dean
Mr. Chas. Gilbert Dean
581 Mr. Jason H. Greenstreet
Mrs. Jason H. Greenstreet
Miss Flora V. Greenstreet
Mr. Chas. Jason Greenstreet
597 Mr. Ivan N. Walker
Mrs. Ivan N. Walker
Mr. Layton C. Walker
Miss Sara J. Walker
600 Mrs. Katharine Lilly
Miss Lilly
Mr. Chas. Lilly
Mrs. Chas. Lilly
621 Miss Grace Gilman Babb
Mrs. Harriet Barbour
Mrs. Anna B. Morrison

631 Mr. Henry L. Browning
Mrs. Henry L. Browning
Miss Eliza G. Browning
Dr. Wm. J. Browning
799 Mr. Harry G. Coughlen
Mrs. Harry G. Coughlen
800 Mr. Henry N. Speare
Mrs. Henry N. Speare
940 Mr. Thomas Thompson
Mrs. Thomas Thompson
946 Mr. Geo. W. White
Mr. Edwin F. White
Mrs. Edwin F. White
Miss Daisy White
948 Mr. Archibald A. Young
Mrs. Archibald A. Young
961 Mr. Geo. A. Buskirk
Mrs. Geo. A. Buskirk
966 Mr. Nelson J. Hyde
Mrs. Nelson J. Hyde
996 Mr. Percival B. Coffin
Mrs. Percival B. Coffin
1085 Dr. Chapin Burgess
Mrs. Chapin Burgess
1087 Meredith Nicholson
Mrs. Willis Nicholson
1089 Mr. Wm. H. Smythe
Mrs. Wm. H. Smythe
1094 Mr. Daniel G. Williams
Mrs. Daniel G. Williams
1104 Mr. David M. Parry
Mrs. David M. Parry

THE ELITE LIST.

VERMONT STREET, WEST.

71 Mr. Duncan Bacon
    Mrs. Duncan Bacon
81 Miss Bertha Test
82 Mr. Chas. H. Abbet
    Mrs. Chas. H. Abbet
    Ernest Lawrence Abbet

98 Mr. Andrew McIntosh
    Mrs. Andrew McIntosh
    Mr. Chas. D. McIntosh
    Miss Sadie E. McIntosh
    Eva S. McIntosh
284 Mr. Thomas E. Chandler
    Mrs. Thomas E. Chandler

WASHINGTON STREET, EAST.

572 Mr. Paul Bahr
    Mrs. Paul Bahr
    Miss Clara Bahr
    Mr. Max Bahr
583 Mr. Harry W. Aldag
644 Mr. Charles Aldag
    Mrs. Charles Aldag
    Miss Minnie Aldag
    Miss Cora Aldag
645 Mr. T. Piel
    Miss Mary Piel
700 Mr. Wm. Henry Piel
    Mrs. Wm. Henry Piel
706 Mr. Charles Frederick Piel
    Mrs. Charles Frederick Piel

779 Mr. Dwight Fraser
    Mrs. Dwight Fraser
    Miss Anna E. Fraser
781 Miss Helen M. Leonard
794 Dr. Wilson Reed
    Mrs. Wilson Reed
    Mr. Wilson H. Reed
    Mr. Edward H. Reed
808 Dr. Alembert Brayton
    Mrs. Alembert Brayton
1140 Mr. Franklin Taylor
    Mrs. Franklin Taylor
    Miss Mary Taylor
1875 Mr. L. L. Jackson

WEST DRIVE, (W. P.)

8 Mr. James R. Carnahan
    Mrs. James R. Carnahan
    Miss Carnahan
16 Mr. Henry Bliss
    Mrs. Henry Bliss
19 Mr. Page Chapman
21 Mr. Wm. G. Wasson
    Mrs. Wm. G. Wasson
    Miss Bertha E. Wasson

21 Miss Emma Wasson
31 Mr. Alexander C. Ayres
    Mrs. Alexander C. Ayres
    Miss Ida Ayres
43 Mr. Joseph Browne
    Mrs. Joseph Browne
47 Mr. Francis Burt
    Mrs. Francis Burt

WEST STREET, NORTH.

- 12 Mr. Ervin Robbins
  Mrs. Ervin Robbins
  Mr. Earl G. Robbins
  Mrs. Sara Ann Robbins
- 15 Mr. Frank Reynolds
  Mrs. Frank Reynolds
  Miss May Reynolds
  Miss Elizabeth Reynolds
  Miss Ada A. Reynolds
- 22 Dr. Alexander Jameson
  Mrs. Alexander Jameson
- 24 Mr. O. W. Stanley
  Mrs. O. W. Stanley
- 34 Mr. Barclay Walker
  Mrs. Barclay Walker
- 44 Mrs. John A. Holman
  Mr. Silas T. Bowen
  Mrs. Silas T. Bowen
- 77 Mrs. Wm. E. Niblack
  Miss Eliza Niblack
  Miss Sara Niblack
- 82 Mr. Ira D. Grover
  Mrs. Ira D. Grover
  Mr. Arthur B. Grover
  Mrs. Arthur B. Grover
- 313 Mr. David C. Borgundthal
  Mrs. David C. Borgundthal
- 384 Miss Ida Scott

WEST SECOND STREET.

- 34 Mr. Wm. H. Coleman
  Mrs. Wm. H. Coleman
- 36 Mr. Robert Martindale
  Mrs. Robert Martindale
- 72 Mr. George Carter
  Mrs. George Carter
- 76 Mr. Wm. C. Lynn
  Mrs. Wm. C. Lynn
  Chas. Jackson Lynn
- 84 Mr. Aretus Hatch
  Mrs. Aretus Hatch
- 86 Mr. Geo. A. Winsor
  Mrs. Emma Winsor
  Marie Winsor
- 122 Mr. Edward Donley
  Mrs. Edward Donley
  Mr. Wm. C. Donley
  Mrs. Wm. C. Donley

THE ELITE LIST.

WEST WALNUT STREET.

20 Mr. Ernest Matthews
    Mrs. Ernest Matthews
    Mr. Horace S. Matthews
    Wilson M. Matthews
25 Mr. Edward G. Cornelius
    Mrs. Edward G. Cornelius
    Miss Sadie Willis Cornelius
30 Miss Nettie Stewart
74 Thomas J. Christian

76 Mrs. Catherine Holmes
    Ella M. Holmes
    Rose Hanna Holmes
81 Mrs. Lillian Wright Dean
90 Mrs. Helen A. Eaton
    Mr. Elias Jacoby
    Mrs. Elias Jacoby
94 Mr. Frank Helwig
    Mrs. Frank Helwig

WOODRUFF PLACE.

3 Mr. Geo. C. Stevens
    Mrs. Geo. C. Stevens
8 Mr. John P. Patterson
11 Mrs. Susan Shedd
    Mr. Edwin H. Shedd
12 Mr. Wm. G. Lockwood
    Mrs. Wm. G. Lockwood
    Miss Margaret Lockwood
13 Mr. Frederick K. Shepard
    Mrs. Frederick K. Shepard
17 Dr. Thomas Hacker
    Mrs. Thomas Hacker
19 Mr. Albert D. Thomas
    Mrs. Albert D. Thomas
21 Mr. John Lewis Griffiths
    Mrs. John Lewis Griffiths
30 Dr. John R. Hussey
    Mrs. John R. Hussey
38 Mr. Evan C. Thomas
    Mrs. Evan C. Thomas

38 Mr. James E. Thomas
    Mrs. James E. Thomas
    Mr. Evan C. Thomas
    Harry Edwin Thomas
39 Mrs. Lizzie Potts
    Mr. Edward G. Potts
    Mrs. Carrie L. Hall
45 Mr. Perley B. Raymond
    Mrs. Perley B. Raymond
47 Mr. Walter Davidson
50 Mr. Percival C. Hord
    Miss Bessie F. Hord
    Miss Mary Hord
    Mr. Wm. P. Hord
    Mr. Horace Hord
    Mrs. Emma B. Hord
54 Mr. Le Grand H. Payne
    Mrs. Le Grand H. Payne
59 Mr. Geo. Raschig
    Mrs. Geo. Raschig

WOODRUFF PLACE.—Continued.

67	Mr. Alfred F. McCormick	103	Mr. John D. Morris
	Mrs. Alfred F. McCormick		Mrs. John D. Morris
75	Mr. John Miller Kerper	115	Mrs. Chas. F. Keller
	Mrs. John Miller Kerper	157	Mr. Noble B. McKee
	Miss Kerper		Mrs. Noble B. McKee
	Miss Mabell Kerper	159	Mr. John F. Messick
77	Mr. Chas. H. Wellner		Mrs. John F. Messick
	Mrs. Chas. H. Wellner	182	Mr. Geo. E. Field
98	Mr. Chas. Edward Test		Mrs. Geo. E. Field
	Mrs. Chas. Edward Test		

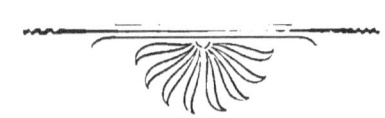

The undersigned announces that he has enlarged his Steel and Copper Plate Engraving & Printing Departments, *and is fully equipped to furnish* Visiting Cards, Wedding and Party Invitations, Monograms, Coats of Arms, Crests & Address Dies, *promptly and in the most approved styles and respectfully solicits your patronage. Samples sent on application.*

Wm. B. Burford,
21 West Washington St.
Indianapolis, Ind.

No. 17, Mrs.

No 16, Miss or Mrs.

No. 15, Miss.

No. 14, Mr. and Mrs.

No. 13, Mrs. (Oblong.)

No. 12, Mr. (Large.)

No. 11, Mr.

No. 10, Mr.

Latest Styles of Engraving

1. Dr. Henry L. Bankring.
2. Mr. Samuel K. Hawley.
3. Mrs. Thomas W. Cummings.
4. Miss Amanda W. Rockwell.
5. Mr. Augustus L. Morgan.
6. Franklin S. Danworth
7. Miss Hendrickson
8. Mr. Edward C. Bulkark
9. Mr. Peter C. Irvington
10. Mr. Nathan G. Banks
11. Charles W. Archindale
12. Miss Ann J. Wright.

*WE DO ALL OUR
OWN WORK IN*

Steel and Copper Plate
Engraving and Printing.

Orders for Visiting Cards, Wedding and Party Invitations, Monograms Coats of Arms, Crests and Address Dies, are filled in our establishment, thus avoiding the delay caused by ordering from other cities.

The Latest Styles and Full Stock of Plain and Fancy Stationery, Folders, Menues, Dance Programs, etc., always on hand.

First-class work and Satisfaction guaranteed in every instance. Samples furnished on application.

WM. B. BURFORD,

21 W. WASHINGTON ST.,
INDIANAPOLIS.

Clubs, Associations

... AND ...

Charitable Institutions.

THE ELITE LIST.

CENTURY CLUB.

OFFICERS.

President:
    EVANS WOOLLEN.
Vice-Presidents:
    LAWSON M. HARVEY,
    WILLIAM C. BOBBS,
    ERNEST R. KEITH.
Secretary:
    ALLAN HENDRICKS.
Treasurer:
    JAMES W. FESLER.

MEMBERS.

Alexander C. Ayres
Charles P. Benedict
Ernest P. Bicknell
Jesse H. Blair
William C. Bobbs
Arthur V. Brown
Edgar A. Brown
Hilton U. Brown
William W. Buchanan
John A. Butler
Scot Butler
Vincent G. Clifford
Linton A. Cox
Millard F. Cox
Frank G. Darlington
Jacob P. Dunn
William F. Elliott
Charles E. Ferguson
James W. Fesler
William Fortune
William S. Garber
Francis H. Gavisk
Louis H. Gibson
John L. Griffiths
Arthur B. Grover
Lawson M. Harvey

THE ELITE LIST.

Allan Hendricks
Thomas E. Hibben
Jacquelin S. Holliday
Charles E. Holloway
Francis T. Hord
James P. Hornaday
Hewitt H. Howland
Alexander Jameson
Alexander Johnson
Richard O. Johnson
F. Rollin Kautz
John L. Ketcham
Ernest R. Keith
James M. Leathers
Virgil H. Lockwood
George L. Mackintosh
Claude Matthews
Allison Maxwell
Joshua V. McNeal
Charles W. Merrill
James L. Mitchell, Jr

Charles W. Moores
Merrill Moores
Laz. Noble
John H. Oliver
Joseph W. Piercy
Edward B. Porter
Alfred F. Potts
Albert Rabb
Halstead L. Ritter
John E. Scott
Russell M. Seeds
Louis A. Share
James Smith
Lucius B. Swift
Harold Taylor
William L. Taylor
Charles N. Thompson
William W. Thornton
Newton Todd
John R. Wilson
Evans Woollen

HONORARY MEMBERS.

James Whitcomb Riley

NON-RESIDENT MEMBERS.

Walter H. Evans, Washington, D. C.
Rice Vance Hunter, Terre Haute, Indiana.
George A. Reisner, Cambridge, Mass.

Lee Travers, Chicago, Ill.
Edward P. Whallon, Cincinnati, Ohio.
Edward P. Whittemore, Toledo, Ohio.

PRESIDENTS.

Eighteen Eighty-Nine - ALFRED F. POTTS.
Eighteen Ninety   - - JACOB P. DUNN.
Eighteen Ninety-One   - WM. F. ELLIOTT.
Eighteen Ninety-Two   - WM. FORTUNE.
Eighteen Ninety-Three - EVANS WOOLLEN.

CLIO CLUB.

OFFICERS.

President:
 FANNIE A. WEBB.
Vice-President:
 ALICE R. TAYLOR.
Secretary:
 KATE P. HARVEY.
Treasurer:
 ANNA C. PYLE.

MEMBERS.

Mrs. Thirza J. Anderson
Mrs. Marietta P. Adams
Mrs. Rosa E. Brown
Mrs. Elizabeth H. Cox
Mrs. Lucy V. B. Coffin
Mrs. Nora Evans
Mrs. Fannie L. Edwards
Mrs. Hannah Furnas
Mrs. Elizabeth N. Hadley
Miss Elsie Hadley
Mrs. Elva W. Hadley
Mrs. Adaline Hollowell
Mrs. Delitha B. Harvey
Mrs. Kate P. Harvey
Mrs. Marianna Hollingsworth
Mrs. Helena K. Harper
Mrs. Cora H. Lane
Mrs. Elizabeth C. Marmon
Mrs. Ella McCrea
Mrs. Lucretia McDowell
Mrs. Luella Nordyke
Miss Clara E. Pray
Miss Anna C. Pyle
Mrs. Anna Risk
Mrs. Maria C. Stubbs
Mrs. Huldah Timberlake
Mrs. Alice R. Taylor
Mrs. Caroline M. Wright
Mrs. Fannie A. Webb
Mrs. Eldora J. C. Witt

COLLEGE CORNER CLUB.

ORGANIZED 1871.

OFFICERS.

President:
JOHN B. ELAM.

Secretary:
J. B. ROBERTS.

THE CONTEMPORARY CLUB.

OFFICERS.

President:
NATHANIEL A. HYDE.
First Vice-President:
SCOT BUTLER.
Second Vice-President:
MRS. JOHN E. CLELAND.
Third Vice-President:
MATTHIAS L. HAINES.
Secretary:
THEODORE L. SEWALL.
Treasurer:
JOHN N. HURTY.

MEMBERS.

Miss Georgia Alexander
Mr. and Mrs. Geo. F. Adams
Mr. and Mrs. Elias C. Atkins
Mr. Henry C. Atkins
Mr. and Mrs. Albert Baker
Miss Nancy Baker
Mr. and Mrs. J. H. Baldwin
Mr. and Mrs. Hervey Bates
Mr. and Mrs. Hervey Bates, Jr
Mr. and Mrs. James B. Black
Mr. and Mrs. F. H. Blackledge
Miss Irene L. Blackledge

Mr. Louis J. Blaker
Mrs. Eliza A. Blaker
Dr. and Mrs. A. W. Brayton
Prof. Demarchus Brown
Mr. and Mrs. Hilton U. Brown
Mr. and Mrs. Chauncey Butler
Mr. and Mrs. Noble C. Butler
Pres. and Mrs. Scot Butler
Miss Georgia E. Butler
Mr. and Mrs. Addison Bybee
Miss Zee Beatty
Mr. and Mrs. C. B. Clarke

Mr. and Mrs. John E. Cleland
Rev. Horace A. Cleveland
Mr. and Mrs. Henry Coburn
Miss Melle Colgan
Miss Macy Coughlen
Pres. and Mrs. J. M. Coulter
Miss N. Cropsey
Mr. and Mrs. Edward Daniels
Mr. and Mrs. Thomas C. Day
Miss Mary Dean
Mr. John C. Dean
Mrs. Lillian Wright Dean
Mr. Wilfred R. Dean
Mrs. David Dennis
Miss Anna Dunlop
Mr. John S. Duncan
Mr. and Mrs. Jacob P. Dunn
Mr. and Mrs. John B. Elam
Mr. Edward C. Elder
Mr. and Mrs. Wm. L. Elder
Mr. William F. Elliott
Mr. and Mrs. C. W. Fairbanks
Dr. and Mrs. C. E. Ferguson
Mr. John A. Finch
Mr. and Mrs. Wm. P. Fishback
Mr. and Mrs. Allen M. Fletcher
Miss Emily Fletcher
Dr. and Mrs. Wm. B. Fletcher
Miss Ruth Fletcher
Mr. and Mrs. Chapin C. Foster
Mr. and Mrs. Wm. D. Foulke

Mr. and Mrs. Louis H. Gibson
Mr. and Mrs. John L. Griffiths
Rev. and Mrs. M. L. Haines
Mr. and Mrs. Hugh H. Hanna
Mr. and Mrs. Clinton L. Hare
Hon. Benjamin Harrison
Mr. Allan W. Hendricks
Miss Bessie Hendricks
Miss Caroline B. Hendricks
Mr. and Mrs. V. K. Hendricks
Mrs. Helen B. Holman
Mr. and Mrs. John H. Holliday
Dr. and Mrs. Edw. F. Hodges
Miss Caroline H. Howland
Miss Elizabeth G. Hughes
Dr. and Mrs. John N. Hurty
Rev. and Mrs. Nath. A. Hyde
Dr. and Mrs. Henry Jameson
Mr. and Mrs. Ovid B. Jameson
Mr. and Mrs. Lewis H. Jones
Mrs. John M. Judah
Mr. and Mrs. Wm. P. Kappes
Mr. and Mrs. John L. Ketcham
Dr. and Mrs. Edwin R. Lewis
Mrs. Margaret V. Marshall
Mr. and Mrs. Chas. Martindale
Mrs. Amanda L. Mason
Mr. and Mrs. August. L. Mason
Miss Hester McClung
Mr. and Mrs. Wm. J. McKee
Mrs. Virginia C. Meredith

Miss Catherine Merrill
Mr. and Mrs. Chas. W. Merrill
Mr. and Mrs. George Merritt
Prof. and Mrs. A. B. Milford
Mr. and Mrs. H. J. Milligan
Dr. James B. Milligan
Miss Deborah D. Moore
Miss Julia H. Moore
Mrs. Mary Sharpe Moore
Mr. Charles W. Moores
Mr. Oliver T. Morton
Miss Anna G. Nicholas
Mr. Meredith Nicholson
Prof. Harriet Noble
Mr. Lazarus Noble
Mr. and Mrs. Oran Perry
Miss Amelia Waring Platter
Hon. Albert G. Porter
Mr. and Mrs. Edw. B. Porter
Mr. George T. Porter
Mr. and Mrs. Alfred F. Potts
Mr. and Mrs. Julius F. Pratt
Miss Laura Ream
Mr. and Mrs. Wm. J. Richards
Mr. James Whitcomb Riley
Mr. Halstead L. Ritter
Mrs. Myla F. Ritzinger
Miss Corinna E. Robbins
Mr. and Mrs. Morris M. Ross
Mr. Theodore L. Sewall
Mrs. May Wright Sewall
Miss Belle M. Sharpe
Pres. and Mrs. Jas. H. Smart
Prof. Alexander Smith
Mr. and Mrs. Alph. H. Snow
Mr. and Mrs. A. P. Spruance
Mr. and Mrs. A. P. Stanton
Mr. and Mrs. T. L. Sullivan
Mr. and Mrs. T. C. Steele
Dr. Rachel Swain
Mr. and Mrs. Lucius B. Swift
Mrs. Elizabeth C. Talbott
Mr. William H. Talbott
Mr. and Mrs. J. S. Tarkington
Mr. and Mrs. M. E. Vinton
Mr. and Mrs. David Wallace
Mr. and Mrs. C. R. Williams
Mr. and Mrs. John R. Wilson
Miss Elizabeth Wishard
Dr. William N. Wishard
Prof. James A. Woodburn
Mr. Evans Woollen

INDIANAPOLIS
CONGREGATIONAL CLUB.

OFFICERS.

President:
W. F. BRUNNER.
First Vice-President:
REV. J. H. CRUM, D. D.
Second Vice-President:
REV. F. E. DEWHURST.
Secretary,
REV. E. S. SMITH.
Treasurer:
W. S. RAWLS.
Auditor:
REV. JOHN HARDEN.

CHARTER MEMBERS.

Prof. W. A. Bell
C. J. Buchanan
Chas. H. Badger
James G. Black
W. H. Burton
W. F. Brunner
Rev. J. H. Crum, D. D.

Rev. E. D. Curtis, D. D.
H. G. Coldwell
Chas. H. Cramer
Rev. F. E. Dewhurst
George L. Davis
Frank B. Fowler
Rev. W. C. Gordon

THE ELITE LIST.

Chas. H. Gillette
Chas. S. Grout
Rev. N. A. Hyde, D. D.
Rev. John Harden
C. E. Hollenbeck
J. R. Irving
E. L. Irving
Rev. F. E. Knopf
S. S. Moore
Frank W. Olin

Thomas H. Perry
W. S. Rawls
Dr. O. S. Runnels.
Prof. J. B. Roberts
Rev. E. S. Smith
E. E. Stacy
Rev. J. W. Wilson
A. B. Willard
H. L. Whitehead

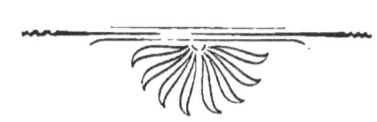

THE DRAMATIC CLUB.

OFFICERS.

BOARD OF DIRECTORS.

President:
MR. MORRIS ROSS.
Vice-President:
MRS. J. ALFRED BARNARD.
Secretary:
MISS CHARLOTTE ELLIOTT JONES.
Treasurer:
MR. HEWITT H. HOWLAND.

MR. JOSEPH BROWN MANSUR.
MR. JOSEPH K. SHARPE, JR.
MISS KATHERINE WALLICK.
MRS. HAROLD TAYLOR.
MISS NANCY NEWCOMER.

MEMBERS.

Miss Mary S. Allen
Miss Mary E. Armstrong
Mr. Henry C. Atkins
Miss Emma Ayres
Miss Florence Baker
Miss Nancy Baker
Miss Anna Belle Baldwin
Mr. Frank M. Baldwin
Mrs. Frank M. Baldwin
Miss Margaret Baldwin
Mr. J. Alfred Barnard
Mrs. J. Alfred Barnard
Miss Margaret G. Barry
Mr. Hervey Bates, Jr.
Mrs. Hervey Bates, Jr.
Mr. Henry W. Bennett

THE ELITE LIST.

Mrs. Henry W. Bennett
Mr. L. H. Blanton
Mr. Duane Bowles
Mr. Joseph M. Bowles
Mr. John Edward Bradshaw
Mr Wm. J. Brown
Mrs. Wm. J. Brown
Miss Lillian Butler
Mr. John A. Butler
Mr. John Maurice Butler
Miss Mary Browning Butler
Mr. Arthur Byfield
Mr. Sam C. Carey
Mr. John Chislett
Miss Jessie L. Clippinger
Mr. Augustus Coburn
Mr. William H. Coburn
Miss Mary E. Colgan
Mr. Samuel Herbert Collins
Mrs. Samuel Herbert Collins
Miss Macy Coughlen
Mr. James B. Curtis
Mrs. James B. Curtis
Mr. Frank Graef Darlington
Mrs. Frank Graef Darlington
Miss Suzette Merrill Davis,
Mr. Howard Albert Dill,
Mrs. Howard Albert Dill
Miss Agnes Duncan
Mr. Jacob P. Dunn
Miss Elizabeth F. Dye

Miss Marie B. Dye
Mr. Wm. H. Dye
Mrs. Wm. H. Dye
Mr. Edward C. Elder
Mr. Wm. L. Elder
Mrs. Wm. L. Elder
Mr. William F. Elliott
Mr. Herbert Emery
Mrs. Herbert Emery
Miss Caroline H. Farquhar
Mr. Jesse Fletcher
Miss Ruth Fletcher
Mr. Henry Scot Fraser
Mrs. Henry Scot Fraser
Miss Amelia Love Gaston
Miss Grace Gaston
Miss Olive Gaston
Mr. W. F. C. Golt
Miss Jane Graydon
Miss Julia Moores Graydon
Mr. Otto Gresham
Mr. John L. Griffiths
Mrs. John L. Griffiths
Mr. Arthur Bradford Grover
Mrs. Arthur Bradford Grover
Mr. Edwin A. Hallam
Mr. Clinton L. Hare
Mrs. Clinton L. Hare
Mr. Allan Hendricks
Mr. William Pirtle Herod
Mrs. William Pirtle Herod

THE ELITE LIST.

Mr. J. S. Holliday
Miss Bessie F. Hord
Mr. Horace Hord
Mr. Percy C. Hord
Mr. Hewitt H. Howland
Mrs. Hewitt H. Howland
Miss Mary Elaine Hussey
Mr. Ovid Butler Jameson
Mrs. Ovid Butler Jameson
Miss Charlotte Elliott Jones
Mr. Wm. White Knight
Mrs. Wm. White Knight
Miss Mary Knippenberg
Mr. Wm. F. Landers
Mr. James F. Leathers
Miss Katharine Lewis
Mr. Alvin S. Lockhard
Miss Carrie Malott
Miss Florence Malott
Miss Katharine Malott
Mr. Joseph Brown Mansur
Mrs. Joseph Brown Mansur
Mr. Charles Martindale
Mrs. Charles Martindale
Miss Emma Martindale
Mr. Lynn B. Martindale
Mr. Robert Martindale
Mrs. Robert Martindale
Mr. Augustus L. Mason
Miss Georgia Maxwell
Mr. Marvin R. Maxwell

Mr. Frank L. McKee
Mr. Charles White Merrill
Mrs. Charles White Merrill
Miss Deborah Duane Moore
Miss Julia Harrison Moore
Mr. Charles W. Moores
Mr. Merrill Moores
Mr. Oliver T. Morton
Miss Nancy I. Newcomer
Mr. Benjamin Nichols
Miss Margaret E. Nicholson
Mr. Meredith Nicholson
Mr. Laz. Noble
Dr. John H. Oliver
Mrs. John H. Oliver
Miss Annie Peck
Miss Lois Josephine Peirce
Mr. John O. Perrin
Mrs. John O. Perrin
Miss Annie Porter
Mr. George T. Porter
Miss Elizabeth Ray
Miss Lillian Reeves
Mr. James Whitcomb Riley
Miss Josephine Robinson
Mr. Morris Ross
Mrs. Morris Ross
Mr. Edward S. R. Seguin
Mrs. Edward S. R. Seguin
Mr. Joseph K. Sharpe, Jr
Mrs. Joseph K. Sharpe, Jr

THE ELITE LIST.

Miss May Louise Shipp
Miss Claire A. Shover
Mr. Alpheus H. Snow
Mrs. Alpheus H. Snow
Mr. Henry Spann
Mr. Wm. Houston Talbott
Mr. N. Booth Tarkington
Mr. Harold Taylor
Mrs. Harold Taylor
Mr. William M. Taylor
Dr. Daniel A. Thompson
Mr. Samuel A. Townsend
Mrs. Samuel A. Townsend
Mr. Benjamin D. Walcott
Mrs. Benjamin D. Walcott
Miss Adele Wallick
Miss Katherine Wallick

Miss Mary Glenn Wallick
Mr. Albert Leaming Willard
Mr. Walter O. Williams
Mr. John R. Wilson
Mrs. John R. Wilson
Miss Sue Winter
Mr. Edson T. Wood
Mr. Willis G. Wood
Miss Alice N. Woods
Mr. Evans Woollen
Mr. James T. Wright
Mrs. James T. Wright
Mr. Clarence Wulsin
Mrs. Clarence Wulsin
Miss Suzanne Van Valkenberg
Mr. Geo. B. Yandes

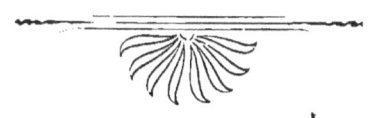

FORTNIGHTLY LITERARY CLUB.

OFFICERS.

President,
HANNAH M. CLAYPOOL.
Vice-President,
ALICE FINCH.
Second Vice-President,
CARRIE MACEY MALOTT.
Recording Secretary,
ALICE BAKER.
Corresponding Secretary,
CORNELIA C. FAIRBANKS.
Treasurer,
LAURA REAM.

MEMBERS.

Miss Fredonia Allen
Mrs. H. C. Allen
Mrs. Albert Baker
Miss Alice Baker
Mrs. J. H. Baldwin
Miss Emily Bingham
Miss Julia A. Brown
Mrs. William J. Brown
Mrs. John R. Brown
Mrs. Chester Bradford
Mrs. Solomon Claypool
Miss Mary Alice Claypool

Mrs. A. L. Claypool
Mrs. Adelia Coe
Mrs. Edward Daniels
Mrs. E. H. Dean
Mrs. Austin Denny
Mrs. John T. Dye
Miss Elizabeth Dye
Miss Marie B. Dye
Mrs. Helen A. Eaton
Mrs. Henry Eitel
Mrs. C. W. Fairbanks
Miss Alice Finch

THE ELITE LIST. 147

Mrs. W. B. Fletcher
Mrs. Horace Fletcher
Mrs. Sarah C. Gill
Mrs. John L. Griffiths
Mrs. W. E. Hackedorn
Mrs. J. W. Hess
Mrs. Wilbur Hitt
Mrs. E. Jacoby
Mrs. Ovid B. Jameson
Mrs. Joseph S. Jenckes
Miss Charlotte E. Jones
Mrs. V. T. Malott

Miss Florence Malott
Miss Kate Malott
Mrs. Claude Matthews
Mrs. J. C. Norris
Mrs. Albert Rabb
Miss Elizabeth Ray
Miss Laura Ream
Mrs. George E. Swan
Mrs. J. S. Tarkington
Mrs. R. D. Townsend
Mrs. Wm. A. VanBuren
Miss Camilla Walker

HONORARY MEMBERS.

Mrs. Charlotte Baker
Mrs. Catherine Bullard
Mrs. H. J. Craft

Mrs. J. W. Holcomb
Mrs. Emma Carleton
Mrs. C. E. Henderson

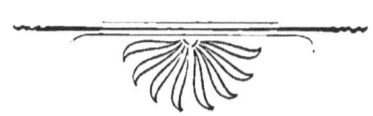

THE KATHARINE MERRILL CLUB.

OFFICERS.

President,
MARY COBURN.

Vice-President,
MARY P. BAKER.

Recording Secretary,
NELLIE D. WILSON.

Corresponding Secretary,
MARY COOK.

Treasurer,
MINA MERRILL.

MEMBERS.

Mrs. H. R. Allen
Mrs. James P. Baker
Mrs. Hervey Bates
Mrs. W. C. Bobbs
Mrs. Hilton U. Brown
Mrs. Scot Butler
Miss Cipriani
Mrs. Charles B. Clarke
Mrs. John E. Cleland
Mrs. Henry Coburn
Miss Henri Colgan
Miss Melle Colgan
Mrs. William Cook
Miss Macy Coughlen
Mrs. F. A. W. Davis
Miss Margaret Day
Mrs. Katharine L. Dorsey
Mrs. L. H. Dunning.
Mrs. Allen M. Fletcher
Mrs. Clarence Forsythe
Mrs. Louis H. Gibson
Miss Ellen Graydon
Miss Anna Griffith
Miss Martha L. Griffith
Mrs. John L. Griffiths
Mrs. Ira D. Grover
Mrs. Wright Hadley
Miss Margaret Hamilton

THE ELITE LIST.

Mrs. Hugh Hanna
Mrs. O. H. Hasselman
Mrs. Walter Hobbs
Mrs. John A. Holman
Miss Selma Ingersoll
Miss Mary Ingersoll
Miss Henri Ingersoll
Mrs. John M. Judah
Mrs. J. L. Ketcham
Mrs. Hugh McK. Landon
Miss Kate Layman
Mrs. Margaret V. Marshall
Mrs. A. B. McGregory
Miss Catharine Merrill
Miss Mina Merrill
Mrs. Charles W. Merrill
Mrs. Frank R. Miller
Miss Lavalette Miller

Miss Julia H. Moore
Miss Harriet Noble
Mrs. J. H. Oliver
Mrs. Alfred F. Potts
Mrs. J. F. Pratt
Miss Josephine Robinson
Miss Harriet Scott
Miss Belle M. Sharpe
Miss May Louise Shipp
Mrs. A. H. Snow
Mrs. Franklin Taylor
Miss Mary Taylor
Mrs. Wm. M. Taylor
Miss Kate Thompson
Mrs. Harriet A. Van Buren
Miss Ruama Wales
Mrs. John R. Willson
Mrs. James T. Wright

CORRESPONDING MEMBERS.

Miss Katharine M. Graydon
Mrs. Mary John
Miss Susan M. Ketcham
Mrs. E. H. Lamme

Miss Mary Merrill
Mrs. Brainard Rorison
Miss Ellen Thompson

INDIANAPOLIS LITERARY CLUB.

OFFICERS.

President:
 NOBLE C. BUTLER.
Vice-Presidents:
 ALBERT J. BEVERIDGE,
 JOHN E. CLELAND,
 AUGUSTUS L. MASON.
Secretary:
 CHARLES EVANS.
Treasurer:
 JOHN N. HURTY.

MEMBERS.

Albert Baker
John A. Baker
William A. Bell
Albert J. Beveridge
James B. Black
Frank H. Blackledge
Alembert W. Brayton
Charles E. Brooks
Demarchus Brown
Hilton U. Brown
Noble C. Butler
Scot Butler
Smiley N. Chambers
Solomon Claypool

John E. Cleland
Horace A. Cleveland
Junius E. Cravens
Edward Daniels
John C. Dean
John T. Dye
Hanford A. Edson
John B. Elam
Byron K. Elliott
William F. Elliott
Charles E. Emmerich
Charles Evans
Charles W. Fairbanks
Charles E. Ferguson

John A. Finch
William P. Fishback
William D. Foulke
Elmer E. Griffith
John L. Griffiths
Matthias L. Haines
Hugh H. Hanna
Addison C. Harris
Edward F. Hodges
John H. Holliday
William DeM. Hooper
John N. Hurty
Nathaniel A. Hyde
Joseph S. Jenckes
L. H. Jones
William A. Ketcham
Harvey M. LaFollette
John Lawrie
Edwin R. Lewis
James E. McCullough
Charles Martindale
Augustus L. Mason
Joseph A. Milburn

Harry J. Milligan
Oliver T. Morton
Meredith Nicholson
Alfred M. Ogle
Robert B. F. Peirce
George T. Porter
Theodore Potter
J. Hilliard Ranger
Junius B. Roberts
Orange S. Runnels
Theodore L. Sewall
Alpheus H. Snow
Theodore C. Steele
Thomas L. Sullivan
Lucius B. Swift
William F. Taylor
J. Livingston Thompson
A. L. Varney
C. F. R. Wappenhans
John R. Wilson
William A. Woods
Evans Woollen

HONORARY MEMBERS.

William F. Abbott
D. S. Alexander
Isaac Arnold
Alvin F. Bailey

John Baltzley
William M. Barr
William A. Bartlett
Allen R. Benton

John M. Bloss
Blanche K. Bruce
Augustus H. Carrier
Joseph B. Cleaver
Clifton Comly
Charles E. Dickinson
Albert E. Fletcher
William A. Geers
William P. Gould
Willard W. Grant
Walter Q. Gresham
Elijah W. Halford
Benjamin Harrison
Lawrence G. Hay
Cyrus C. Hines
Willard H. Hinkley
John W. Holcombe
Ross C. Houghton
Louis Howland
J. Henry Kappes
John A. Kress
J. Augustus Lemcke
Augustus D. Lynch

James McLeod
Edward B. Mason
Samuel Merrill
William H. H. Miller
Theophilus Parvin
Asa G. Pettibone
Albert G. Porter
Myron W. Reed
William H. Rexford
James G. Rodger
John G. Shanklin
Ebenezer Sharpe
Horace Speed
James H. Smart
Jared A. Smith
Horace S. Tarbell
Arthur W. Tyler
Henry H. Walker
John H. Warder
David C. Wells
Edward P. Whalon
George B. Wright

HONORARY MEMBERS
BY ELECTION.

John Merle Coulter
David Starr Jordan

James Whitcomb Riley

INDIANAPOLIS PROPYLÆUM.

OFFICERS.

President:
 HELEN B. HOLMAN.
Vice-President:
 HARRIET MACINTIRE FOSTER.
Recording Secretary:
 ANNIE AMES SPRUANCE.
Corresponding Secretary:
 MARY COBURN ALLEN.
Treasurer:
 MARGARETTA S. ELDER.

MEMBERS.

Mrs. W. B. Allen
Mrs. E. C. Atkins
Mrs. Eliza C. Bell
Mrs. Pleasant Bond
Miss Emily S. Bingham
Mrs. Kate M. Bowles
Mrs. F. H. Blackledge
Miss Georgiana Butler
Mrs. Scot Butler
Mrs. H. G. Carey
Mrs. John N. Carey
Mrs. Lowe Carey
Mrs. George H. Chapman
Mrs. F. W. Chislett

Mrs. Smiley N. Chambers
Mrs. John E. Cleland
Mrs. Henry Coburn
Mrs. Linton A. Cox
Mrs. K. L. Dorsey
Mrs. James T. Eaglesfield
Mrs. Hanford A. Edson
Miss Alice Edwards
Mrs. John B. Elam
Miss Margaretta S. Elder
Mrs. William Line Elder
Miss Emily Fletcher
Mrs. Horace H. Fletcher
Miss Ruth Fletcher

Mrs. Chapin C. Foster
Mrs. Charles E. Hall
Mrs. Otto H. Hasselman
Mrs. Watson J. Hasselman
Mrs. Theo. P. Haughey
Miss Anna Hendricks
Miss Eliza S. Hendricks
Mrs. Victor K. Hendricks
Mrs. George C. Hitt
Mrs. Edward F. Hodges
Mrs. John H. Holliday
Mrs. John A. Holman
Miss Caroline H. Howland
Mrs. Geo. W. Hufford
Mrs. N. A. Hyde
Mrs. Henry Jameson
Mrs. Ovid B. Jameson
Mrs. W. A. Ketcham
Mrs. J. L. Ketcham
Mrs. Oscar C. McCulloch
Mrs. A. B. McGregory
Mrs. Martha N. McKay
Mrs. Margaret V. Marshall
Mrs. Henry C. Martin
Mrs. Charles Martindale
Miss Catharine Merrill
Mrs. Joseph A. Milburn

Mrs. H. J. Milligan
Miss Janet D. Moores
Mrs. Julia M. Moores
Miss Julia Harrison Moore
Miss Anna Nicholas
Miss Elizabeth Nicholson
Miss Harriet Noble
Mrs. Henry D. Pierce
Miss Marie Ritzinger
Mrs. A. M. Robertson
Mrs. Morris M. Ross
Mrs. Theo. L. Sewall
Miss Belle M. Sharpe
Mrs. John M. Spann
Mrs. Alexander P. Spruance
Mrs. J. H. Stewart
Mrs. George G. Tanner
Miss Mary L. Taylor
Mrs. Merrick E. Vinton
Mrs. Theodore A. Wagner
Mrs. Benj. D. Walcott
Mrs. Graham A. Wells
Mrs. Eliza G. Wiley
Mrs. James M. Winters
Mrs. William Watson Woollen
Mrs. James T. Wright

CORRESPONDING MEMBERS.

Mrs. Gertrude G. Aguirre
Mrs. Susan A. Carrier
Mrs. Mary B. Chislett
Miss Anna Dunlop
Miss Katharine M. Graydon
Mrs. Nora F. Hay
Miss Grettie Y. Holliday
Mrs. Mary Hubbard Johnson
Mrs. Mary Sanders Judah
Mrs. Mary Harrison McKee
Miss Mary Talbott Morrison
Mrs. Arabella C. Peelle
Miss Mary C. Rariden
Mrs. Mary H. Smart
Miss Ellen F. Thompson
Mrs. Maria N. Fulton

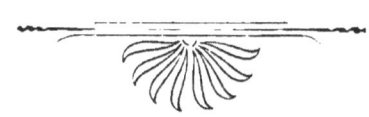

LADIES' MATINEE MUSICALE.

OFFICERS.

President:
  MRS. A. M. ROBERTSON.
Vice-President:
  MRS. HENRY SCHURMANN.
Secretary:
  MRS. WM. C. LYNN.
Corresponding Secretary:
  MRS. J. S. JENCKES.
Treasurer:
  MRS. GEO. F. BRANHAM.
Librarian:
  MISS SARAH T. MEIGS.

MEMBERS.

Mrs. D. F. Appel
Miss Augusta Austin
Mrs. Frederick Baggs
Mrs. Leon O. Bailey
Miss India Barnheiser
Mrs. Anna Wilcox-Barry
Miss Julia Bassett
Mrs. J. W. Beck
Miss Bessie Beck
Mrs. Henry Benham
Miss May Bergenthal
Mrs. G. F. Branham

Miss Nannie Branham
Miss Julia Brown
Miss Lulu Burt
Miss Fannie Carlton
Miss Adelaide Carman
Miss Addie Carter
Mrs. C. E. Coffin
Miss Anna Constant
Mrs. Jessie Applegate-Cost
Miss Macy Coughlen
Mrs. A. G. Cox
Mrs. Annie Robert-Dietrichs

THE ELITE LIST.

Miss Nettie Dietrichs
Mrs. Camilla Walker-Dill
Mrs. Nettie Dillingham
Mrs. M. E. Dooley
Miss Nellie Duncan
Mrs. Clara H. Eddy
Miss Margaretta Elder
Mrs. Benjamin Enos
Miss Juliet Evarts
Miss Anna Farquhar
Miss Belle Ford
Miss Mary Frazee
Mrs. Jacob Friedlich
Mrs. A. B. Gates
Mrs. Clara Wood Glover
Mrs. Louis Gray
Miss Ella Haines
Mrs. Mary Spann-Hanckel
Mrs. U. J. Hammond
Mrs. O. H. Hasselman
Mrs. W. J. Hasselman
Mrs. P. Haughey
Mrs. Ada Heine
Miss Lydia Herron
Miss May Herron
Miss Emma Hill
Mrs. Mary A. Gates-Howland
Miss Ruby Hughes
Mrs. F. M. Hunter
Mrs. Henry Jameson
Miss May Johnson

Mrs. J. S. Jenckes
Mrs. Aquilla Jones
Miss Edith Kahn
Mrs. Burnett Bloomer-Kelsey
Mrs. Flor. Bamberger-Kiser
Mrs. Anna Baggs-Koehne
Miss Mary Leathers
Mrs. Carrie Colver-Leckner
Miss Daisy Lemon
Mrs. Grace D. Levering
Miss Katharine Lewis
Mrs. J. R. Lilley
Mrs. Blanch Dollens-Lilly
Mrs. W. C. Lynn
Mrs. J. A. Lyon
Mrs. Mason
Miss Mary Mather
Miss Angela Maxwell
Miss Jessie Meek
Miss Sarah Meigs
Miss Essie Messing
Mrs. Charles Miller
Miss Clara Miller
Mrs. Enrique C. Miller
Mrs. Winifred Hunter-Mooney
Miss Deborah Moore
Miss Mary Morrison
Mrs Marcia Willard-Morrison
Mrs. Constance Heine-Mozzari
Mrs. S. Mühl
Miss Lavinia McKenna

THE ELITE LIST.

Miss Anna McKenzie
Miss Emily McDowell
Miss Louise New
Miss Alice Newell
Miss Eliza Niblack
Miss Caroline Cooper-Ogle
Mrs. Emma Thompson-Oliver
Mrs. H. O. Pantzer
Mrs. Emma Grooms-Pearson
Mrs. Daisy White-Porter
Miss Harriet Porter
Mrs. Lottie Adam-Raschig
Miss Elizabeth Ray
Mrs. Sidney Reed
Miss Emma Ridenour
Miss Josephine Rittenhouse
Mrs. Amy Willard-Roberts
Miss Mary M. Roberts
Mrs. A. M. Robertson
Miss S. E. Rudisell
Miss Lilian Russell
Miss Louise Schrader
Mrs. Henry Schurmann
Mrs. W. W. Scott
Miss Belle Sharpe
Mrs. Lizzie Walker-Sharpe
Mrs. John M. Shaw
Miss Kate Sheets

Miss Claire Shover
Miss Lucia Sickels
Miss Benaldine Smith
Mrs. W. C. Smock
Mrs. M. H. Spades
Miss Mary Stewart
Miss Mary Stowell
Miss Jennie Suffern
Miss Esther Swain
Miss Ida Sweenie
Miss Louise Sylla
Miss Hautie Tarkington
Miss Caroline Taylor
Mrs. M. L. Thorn
Mrs. Fannie Vajen-Voorhees
Mrs. Anna Walker
Miss Sadie Walker
Miss Adele Wallick
Miss Ida Wallingford
Mrs. C. R. Watson
Miss Bessie West
Mrs. D. L. Whittier
Miss Georgia Whittier
Miss Jessie Whitridge
Miss Riah Wilcox
Miss Winifred Willard
Miss Ray Williams

IN MEMORIAM.

Mrs. U. J. Hammond	1879
Miss Emma Hill	1884
Miss May Bergenthal	1887
Mrs. Constance Heine-Mozzari	1886
Mrs. Minnie Thorn-Lewis	1889
Mrs. Grace D. Levering	1891
Mrs. Rose C. Bailey	1892

THE MINERVA CIRCLE.

OFFICERS.

President:
 MRS. WM. T. BROWN.
  Vice-Presidents:
   MRS. STELLA ANDERSON,
   MRS. JOHN PARIS.
    Recording Secretary:
     MISS JEANNETTE SMITH.
      Corresponding Secretary:
       MRS. J. W. PIERCY.
        Treasurer:
         MISS SARAH RUDISILL.
          Critic:
           MRS. JENNIE BALLENGER.

MEMBERS.

Mrs. Stella Anderson
Mrs. Ernest Bicknell
Mrs. W. T. Brown
Miss Alice Brown
Mrs. Jennie Ballenger
Mrs. J. F. Carson
Miss Viola Flack
Mrs. E. E. Griffith
Miss Jessie Hauck
Mrs. Oscar L. Huey
Mrs. Frank McAlpine
Mrs. Philip E. Mutchner
Mrs. John W. Paris
Mrs. J. W. Piercy
Miss Sarah Rudisill
Miss Jeannette Smith
Miss Nancy Warman
Miss Margaret Wells
Mrs. Wm. A. Wildhack

OVER THE TEACUPS.

OFFICERS.

President,
SUE E. H. PERKINS.

Vice-President,
KATHERINE HUNTINGTON DAY.

Secretary,
EVALINE M. HOLLIDAY.

Treasurer,
SARAH W. ALEXANDER.

MEMBERS.

Mrs. Coke Alexander
Mrs. William C. Allen
Mrs. John R. Brown
Mrs. Vinson Carter
Mrs. Robert W. Cathcart
Mrs. Henry Coe
Mrs. Henry T. Conde
Mrs. Thomas C. Day
Mrs. Katherine L. Dorsey
Mrs. Arthur N. Dwyer
Miss Alice Finch
Mrs. Maria M. Finch
Mrs. F. E. Hale
Mrs. John H. Holliday
Mrs. Flora C. Jones
Mrs. John W. Jones
Mrs. L. Anna Mavity
Mrs. Allison Maxwell
Mrs. Frank F. McCrea
Mrs. W. H. H. Miller
Mrs. Elliott Perkins
Mrs. Charles N. Thompson
Mrs. Henry L. Van Hoff
Mrs. Daniel L. Wood
Mrs. William W. Woollen

PARLOR CLUB.

OFFICERS.

President:
MISS ELIZABETH NICHOLSON.
Vice-President:
MRS. STEVENS.
Secretary:
MRS. ELI PERKINS.
Treasurer:
MISS DEARBON.

THE PORTFOLIO.

OFFICERS.

President:
CLARENCE FORSYTH.
Vice-President:
ALEMBERT W. BRAYTON.
Secretary:
JULIA G. SHARPE.
Treasurer:
FREDERICK A. HETHERINGTON.

MEMBERS.

Franz X. Arens
Emma Arens
Cora C. Barnett
John T. Barnett
Joseph M. Bowles
Alembert W. Brayton
Jessie M. Brayton
Demarchus C. Brown
Hilton U. Brown
Jenny H. Brown
Addison Bybee
Mary Bybee
Ada Comingore
George S. Cottman
William H. Donley
Laura J. Donley

Charlotte J. Dunn
Jacob P. Dunn
Agnes B. Fletcher
William B. Fletcher
Clarence Forsyth
Mary L. Forsyth
William Forsyth
Emily S. Gibson
Louis H. Gibson
Allan Hendricks
Bessie Hendricks
Caroline B. Hendricks
Emma B. Hetherington
Frederick A. Hetherington
James B. Heywood
Caroline M. Heywood

Janet K. Hibben
Thomas E. Hibben
C. E. Hollenbeck
William Hunter
Flora M. Hunter
Katherine Layman
Carl H. Lieber
John H. Mahoney
Hugh Th. Miller
Anna Nicholas
Meredith Nicholson
Charles A. Nicoli
Clara G. Nicoli
Daniel L. Paine
Theodore Potter
Julius F. Pratt
Mary S. Pratt

Armin Recker
James Whitcomb Riley
Frances M. Ross
Morris Ross
Bruce Rogers
Julia G. Sharpe
Mary E. Steele
Theodore C. Steele
Adolph Schellschmidt
Emma Schellschmidt
Ida Schliewen
Richard Schliewen
John H. Stem
Booth Tarkington
Alice N. Woods
Harry Williamson
C. J. R. Wappenhans

NON-RESIDENT MEMBERS.

J. O. Adams - - - Muncie, Ind.
Lucy H. Fletcher - - - Palo Alto, Cal.
Albert Fletcher - - - Palo Alto, Cal.
Elizabeth Stevenson - - - New York.
Harriet Stevenson - - New York.

HONORARY MEMBER.
Daniel L. Paine

… THE ELITE LIST.

ART ASSOCIATION.

OFFICERS.

President:
NATHANIEL A. HYDE.
Vice-Presidents:
LOUISA A. WRIGHT, MAY WRIGHT SEWALL,
WILLIAM F. TAYLOR.
Recording Secretary:
INDIA C. HARRIS.
Corresponding Secretary:
LAURA F. HODGES.
Treasurer:
MARY B. HUSSEY.

DIRECTORS.

REBECCA R. ADAMS CARL H. LIEBER
MARY E. BLACKLEDGE AMELIA B. MANSUR
JOSEPH M. BOWLES AUGUSTUS L. MASON
ESTHER M. BRADSHAW EUGENIA B. McOUAT
MARY I. BYBEE MARY S. PRATT
CHARLES E. COFFIN ALICE M. RICHARDS
MARTHA E. LANDERS WILLIAM H. TALBOTT

HONORARY MEMBERS.

Gen. Lewis Wallace Miss Isabel Edgar
Mrs. Lewis Wallace Mr. T. C. Steele
Mrs. Benjamin Harrison Mr. Wm. T. Harris
Mr. William M. Chase

MEMBERS.

Mrs. Bertrand Adams
Mr. George F. Adams
Mrs. George F. Adams
Mrs. D. E. Allen
Dr. E. W. Anderson
Mrs. E. C. Atkins
Mrs. L. S. Ayres
Miss Emma Ayres
Mrs. A. R. Baker
Mrs. G. M. Ballard
Mrs. T. M. Bassett
Mr. Douglass Barkley
Mrs. W. F. Barkley
Mr. J. Alfred Barnard
Mrs. J. Alfred Barnard
Mr. W. T. Barnes
Miss Margaret Barry
Mrs. Hervey Bates
Mrs. J. W. Beck
Mrs. H. W. Bennett
Mrs. A. J. Beveridge
Mrs. H. A. Bingham
Mrs. M. E. Blackledge
Mrs. A. Blitz
Mrs. Frederick Bossler
Mr. J. M. Bowles
Mrs. E. M. Bradshaw
Mrs. J. A. Bradshaw
Mrs. J. W. Bradshaw
Mrs. W. J. Brown

Mrs. W. R. Brown
Miss Mary Bryson
Mrs. Anna Buchanan
Mrs. N. J. Burford
Mrs. Wm. B. Burford
Miss Lillian Butler
Mr. and Mrs. Scot Butler
Mrs. Addison Bybee
Miss Jessie Bybee
Mrs. A. A. Cady
Miss Cora Campbell
Mrs. James R. Carnahan
Mr. George N. Catterson
Mrs. George N. Catterson
Mr. Wm. Chase
Mr. F. W. Chislett
Mrs. F. W. Chislett
Mrs. F. W. Churchman
Miss Anna Churchman
Miss Mary Clark
Mrs. E. F. Claypool
Mrs. Henry Coburn
Mr. Henry Coe
Mrs. Henry Coe
Mr. C. E. Coffin
Mrs. C. E. Coffin
Mrs. David Coffin
Mr. F. A. Coffin
Mrs. F. A. Coffin
Mr. P. B. Coffin

THE ELITE LIST. 167

Mrs. P. B. Coffin
Mr. W. H. Coleman
Mrs. W. H. Coleman
Mrs. H. T. Condé
Miss Corey
Mrs. N. F. Dalton
Mr. Edward Daniels
Mrs. Edward Daniels
Mrs. C. E. Darke
Mr. F. G. Darlington
Mrs. F. G. Darlington
Mr. T. C. Day
Mrs. T. C. Day
Miss Margaret Day
Mr. E. H. Dean
Mrs. E. H. Dean
Mr. John C. Dean
Mrs. John C. Dean
Miss Mary Dean
Mr. Wilfred R. Dean
Mrs. Thomas Dean
Mrs. W. H. Dean
Mrs. A. J. Decker
Mrs. W. O. DeVay
Mr. Chas. J. Doherty
Mrs. K. L. Dorsey
Mrs. F. W. Douglass
Mrs. Harry E. Drew
Mr. W. H. Eastman
Miss Isabel Edgar
Mrs. John R. Elder

Mrs. George Ellis
Mr. D. P. Erwin
Mrs. Geo. T. Evans
Mrs. Frederick Fahnley
Mrs. C. W. Fairbanks
Mrs. Mary Flanner
Mr. Allen Fletcher
Mrs. Allen Fletcher
Dr. C. I. Fletcher
Mrs. C. I. Fletcher
Miss Julia Fletcher
Miss Louise Fletcher
Mr. S. J. Fletcher
Mr. Jesse Fletcher
Miss Ruth Fletcher
Mrs. Howard Foltz
Mr. William Forsythe
Mr. William Fortune
Mrs. C. C. Foster
Mr. Louis H. Gibson
Mrs. Louis H. Gibson
Mr. W. F. C. Golt
Miss Jennie Graydon
Miss Anna Griffith
Mrs. J. L. Griffiths
Mrs. W. C. Griffith
Mrs. I. D. Grover
Mr. Wm. E. Hackedorn
Mrs. Wm. E. Hackedorn
Rev. M. L. Haines
Mrs. M. L. Haines

THE ELITE LIST.

Miss Margaret Hamilton
Mrs. Schuyler C. Haughey
Mrs. Theodore P. Haughey
Mr. Clinton L. Hare
Mrs. Clinton L. Hare
Mrs. M. L. Hare
Mrs. A. C. Harris
Mr. Wm. T. Harris
Mrs. Benjamin Harrison
Miss Bessie Hendricks
Mrs. E. C. Hendricks
Mrs. Victor Hendricks
Miss Mary Heron
Mrs. M. L. Hess
Mr. J. B. Heywood
Mrs. J. B. Heywood
Miss Heywood
Mrs. L. F. Hodges
Mrs. C. E. Hollenbeck
Mr. J. N. Holliday
Mrs. J. N. Holliday
Mrs. W. J. Holliday
Mrs. C. E. Holloway
Mrs. E. J. Holloway
Mrs. Lewis Hollweg
Miss Norman Hollweg
Mr. Charles Holstein
Mrs. Charles Holstein
Dr. John W. Hurty
Mrs. John W. Hurty
Dr. J. R. Hussey

Mrs. J. R. Hussey
Mrs. B. Hutchinson
Rev. N. A. Hyde
Mrs. N. A. Hyde
Miss Josephine Hyde
Mrs. Ovid B. Jameson
Mr. Wm. P. Kappes
Mrs. Wm. P. Kappes
Mr. A. R. King
Miss Emma King
Mrs. John M. Kitchen
Mrs. Henry Knippenberg
Miss Knippenberg
Mrs. Charles Kregelo
Mrs. Franklin Landers
Mrs. Wm. Latham
Mrs. J. F. Lecklider
Mrs. H. H. Lee
Mrs. T. A. Lewis
Miss K. Lewis
Mr. Herman Lieber
Mr. Carl Lieber
Col. Eli Lilly
Mrs. Eli Lilly
Mrs. C. B. Lockard
Mrs. H. C. Long
Mrs. Mary F. Love
Mr. Bement Lyman
Mrs. Bement Lyman
Mrs. A. B. Mansur
Mr. J. B. Mansur

THE ELITE LIST.

Mrs. J. B. Mansur
Mrs. E. B. Martindale
Mr. A. L. Mason
Mrs. W. F. Mason
Mrs. H. C. Martin
Mr. Frank Maus
Mrs. Frank Maus
Mrs. C. E. Merrifield
Rev. J. A. Milburn
Miss Valette Miller
Mrs. H. J. Milligan
Miss Deborah Moore
Miss Julia Moore
Mrs. J. W. Morris
Mr. Nathan Morris
Mrs. N. N. Morris
Mrs. Fanny Morrison
Miss Fanny McCarty
Mrs. Frank McCrea
Mrs. J. E. McCullough
Mrs. J. E. McDonald
Mrs. Horace McKay
Miss Cornelia McKay
Mrs. W. J. McKee
Mrs. Mary McKenzie
Mrs. M. P. McNeal
Mrs. E. B. McOuat
Mrs. A. H. Nordyke
Mr. A. M. Ogle
Mrs. A. M. Ogle
Mrs. M. J. Osgood

Mrs. LeGrand Payne
Mrs. E. A. Peck
Mr. J. R. Pearson
Mrs. J. R. Pearson
Mrs. H. D. Pierce
Miss M. A. Platter
Mr. E. B. Porter
Mrs. E. B. Porter
Mrs. Alfred Potts
Mr. J. F. Pratt
Mrs. J. F. Pratt
Mr. M. F. Randolph
Mrs. M. F. Randolph
Miss Lillie Reese
Major W. J. Richards
Mrs. W. J. Richards
Mrs. G. L. Rittenhouse
Mrs. Myla F. Ritzinger
Miss Julia Ritzinger
Miss Jennie Roache
Mrs. C. F. Robbins
Miss Margaret Robinson
Miss Kate Robson
Miss Alice Ross
Dr. Sollis Runnels
Mrs. Sollis Runnels
Prof. H. L. Rust
Mrs. Charles Sayles
Mr. J. C. Shaffer
Mrs. J. C. Shaffer
Mr. J. N. Schmidt

THE ELITE LIST.

Mrs. Henry Schurman
Mr. Oscar Sears
Mrs. Russell Seeds
Miss Rhoda Selleck
Mrs. Henry Severin
Mr. T. L. Sewall
Mrs. T. L. Sewall
Miss Nellie Simmons
Mr. J. K. Sharpe, Jr
Mrs. J. K. Sharpe, Jr
Miss Julia Sharpe
Mrs. A. H. Snow
Mrs. J. S. Spann
Mr. J. M. Spann
Mrs. J. M. Spann
Mr. T. H. Spann
Mrs. T. H. Spann
Mr. A. P. Stanton
Mrs. A. P. Stanton
Mr. T. C. Steele
Mrs. T. M. Stevens
Mrs. Daniel Stewart
Mrs. J. H. Stewart
Mr. George W. Stout
Mrs. George Sullivan
Dr. Rachel Swain
Mrs. E. C. Talbott
Mr. W. H. Talbott

Rev. W. F. Taylor
Mrs. W. F. Taylor
Mrs. J. L. Thompson
Mr. Newton Todd
Mrs. A. J. Treat
Mrs. M. B. Tuttle
Mr. M. E. Vinton
Mrs. M. E. Vinton
Gen. Lewis Wallace
Mrs. Lewis Wallace
Mrs. Minnie S. Wallace
Mrs. M. A. Warburton
Mrs. J. B. Warne
Mrs. H. P. Wasson
Mrs. Henry Wetzel
Miss Alice Wick
Mrs. Leonard Wilde
Mrs. C. C. Williams
Mrs. M. B. Wilson
Mrs. D. P. Winings
Mr. James M. Winters
Mrs. James M. Winters
Mrs. D. L. Whitten
Mr. John C. Wright
Mrs. John C. Wright
Mrs. W. A. Woods
Miss Alice Woods
Mrs. Clarence Wulsin

FLOWER MISSION.

OFFICERS.

President:
  MRS. VICTORIA K. HENDRICKS.
  Vice-President:
    MRS. W. J. McKEE.
    2d Vice-President:
      MISS AGNES DILKES.
      3d Vice-President:
        MRS. JOHN H. HOLLIDAY.
        Secretary:
          MRS. HERBERT COLLINS.
          Treasurer:
            MISS GERTRUDE GOODHART.

THE ELITE LIST.

BOYS' HOME
AND
EMPLOYMENT ASSOCIATION.

OFFICERS AND DIRECTORS.

President:
   M. V. McGILLIARD.
      Vice-President:
         MISS MARY KNIPPENBERG.
            Secretary and Superintendent:
               S. C. GILMAN.
                  Treasurer:
                     E. G. CORNELIUS.
                       Matron:
                          MRS. J. C. HARDING.

ELI F. RITTER,
   T. C. DAY,
      MRS. J. H. VAJEN,
         CHAS. E. REYNOLDS,
            MISS MARY EAST,
               MRS. SILAS BALDWIN,
                  MRS. F. E. HELWIG,
                     D. L. WHITTIER,
                        GEN. JOHN COBURN,
                           DAVID F. SWAIN.

DEAF AND DUMB ASYLUM.

Superintendent:
RICHARD O. JOHNSON.
Teachers:
DR. WILLIAM LATHAM,
DR. WILLIAM DeMOTTE,
MR. NOBLE B. McKEE,
MR. SIDNEY J. VAIL,
MR. HENRY BIERHAUS,
MR. AUGUST JUTT,
MR. ORSON ARCHIBALD,
MR. ALBERT BERG,
MR. GILBERT,
MR. CHARLES KERNEY,
MR. NATHANIEL FIELD MORROW,
MISS ANNA HENDRICKS,
MISS HEIZER,
MISS EUDORA BRIGHT,
MRS. SADIE J. CORWIN,
MISS IDA BELLE KINSLEY,
MISS MARVIN,
MISS SMITH,
MISS BOOTHE,
MISS MARY CORWIN (Art Teacher.)

INDIANA REFORM SCHOOL FOR GIRLS,
AND
WOMAN'S PRISON.

OFFICERS.

President:
ELIZA C. HENDRICKS.
Secretary:
MARGARETTA S. ELDER.
Superintendent:
SARAH F. KEELY.
Assistant Superintendent:
MRS. ANNA PRETTYMAN.

BOARD OF MANAGERS.

ELIZA C. HENDRICKS, Indianapolis.
CLAIRE A. WALKER, Indianapolis.
LAURA REAM, Indianapolis.

INDUSTRIAL SCHOOL FOR GIRLS.

OFFICERS.

President:
 MRS. FRANK BLANCHARD.
 Vice-President:
 MRS. FRED. JUDSON.
 Treasurer:
 MRS. GEORGE CARTER.
 Secretary:
 MRS. WALTER H. BALLARD.
 Superintendent Primary Dep't:
 MRS. MARY A. BINFORD.

INDIANAPOLIS FREE KINDERGARTEN

AND

CHILDREN'S AID SOCIETY.

OFFICERS.

President:
   MRS. ELIZA G. WILEY.

  Vice-Presidents:
   MRS. J. W. HESS,
   MRS. J. H. BALDWIN,
   MRS. OSCAR C. McCULLOCH,
   MRS. GEORGE E. TOWNLEY.

   Treasurer:
   MRS. CHAS. E. DARK.

   Recording Secretary:
   MRS. JOHN B. ELAM.

   Corresponding Secretary:
   MRS. GEORGE W. HUFFORD.

THE ELITE LIST.

THE KATHARINE HOME.

OFFICERS.

President:
    MRS. T. P. HAUGHEY.
  First Vice-President:
    MRS. J. C. WRIGHT.
    Second Vice-President:
      MRS. C. E. KREGELO.
      Third Vice-President:
        MRS. ALLEN FLETCHER.
Fourth Vice-President:
  MRS. SILAS BALDWIN.
    Recording Secretary:
      MRS. ANNA B. MORRISON.
    Corresponding Secretary:
      MRS. W. R. EVANS.
      Treasurer:
        MRS. CLEMENS VONNEGUT.
        Auditor:
          MRS. A. H. SNOW.

LOCAL COUNCIL OF WOMEN.

OFFICERS.

President:
    MRS. MARGARET D. CHISLETT.
    Corresponding Secretary:
        MRS. MARY COBURN.
        Recording Secretary:
            MISS JULIA HARRISON MOORE.
            Treasurer:
                MRS. ELIZABETH MARMON.

WOMAN'S AUX. TO Y. M. C. A.

OFFICERS.

President:
 MRS. J. C. BUCHANAN.
  Vice-President:
   MRS. F. F. McCREA.
    Secretary:
     MISS R. B. COOK.
      Treasurer:
       MRS. A. A. OGLE.

ADDENDA.

ADDITIONS AND CORRECTIONS TO REGULAR LIST.

Butler Maurice John, Mr..................606 Delaware st.
Coffin David W., Mr. and Mrs..............27 E. Second st.
Dean Lillian Wright, Mrs............571 N. Pennsylvania st.
Douthirt Stephen T., Mr. and Mrs..........Occidental Hotel.
Holloway Charles Edwin, Mrs......844 N. Pennsylvania st.
Hume James, Mr. and Mrs ....80½ N. Pennsylvania st.
Hurty John, Dr. and Mrs ....29 E. Second st.
Jordan Arthur, Mr. and Mrs..............729 N. Meridian St.
Judson Abbey, Mrs....................407 N. Tennessee St.
Leathers James M., Mr........................14 (W. P.)
Mansur Wm., Mr. and Mrs.........80½ N. Pennsylvania st.
McKee Robert S., Mr ....418 N. Tennessee st.
Merrill Charles W., Mr..................418 N. Tennessee st.
Runnels Orange S., Dr...................600 N. Meridian st.
Scherracker H. J., Mr ....
Sewall May Wright, Mrs............343 N. Pennsylvania st.
Share George K., Mr. and Mrs........366 N. Tennessee st.
Vonegut Her and Dr. and Mrs............342 Home ave.

ERRATA. In Alphabetical List "Maxinkucku" should read *"Maxinkuckee."*

www.ingramcontent.com/pod-product-compliance
Lightning Source LLC
Chambersburg PA
CBHW020250170426
43202CB00008B/308